Confirmed in the Spirit

AUTHORS
SISTERS OF NOTRE DAME
CHARDON, OHIO

LOYOLA PRESS.
A JESUIT MINISTRY
Chicago

IMPRIMATUR	IN CONFORMITY
In accordance with c. 827, permission to publish is granted on April 13, 2012 by Rev. Msgr. John F. Canary, Vicar General of the Archdiocese of Chicago. Permission to publish is an official declaration of ecclesiastical authority that the material is free from doctrinal and moral error. No legal responsibility is assumed by the grant of this permission.	The Subcommittee on the Catechism, United States Conference of Catholic Bishops, has found this text, copyright 2014, to be in conformity with the *Catechism of the Catholic Church;* it may be used only as supplemental to other basal catechetical texts.

Grateful acknowledgment is given to authors, publishers, photographers, museums, and agents for permission to reprint the following copyrighted material. Every effort has been made to determine copyright owners. In the case of any omissions, the publisher will be pleased to make suitable acknowledgments in future editions. Acknowledgments continue on page 121.

Advisors: Barbara F. Campbell, M.Div., D.Min.; Jeanette L. Graham, M.A.; Jean Hopman, O.S.U., M.A.
Cover design: Loyola Press
Cover illustrations: Mackey Creations/Shutterstock.com (dove), iStockphoto/Thinkstock (background)
Interior design: Loyola Press

ISBN-13: 978-0-8294-3681-5
ISBN-10: 0-8294-3681-2

Copyright © 2014 Loyola Press, Chicago, Illinois.

Printed in the United States of America.

LOYOLAPRESS.
A JESUIT MINISTRY

3441 N. Ashland Avenue
Chicago, Illinois 60657
(800) 621-1008
www.loyolapress.com

12 13 14 15 16 17 18 19 Web 10 9 8 7 6 5 4 3 2 1

contents

pray

Come, Holy Spirit, fill the hearts of your faithful.

And kindle in them the fire of your love.

Send forth your Spirit and they shall be created.

And you shall renew the face of the earth.

Let us pray:

O God, by the light of the Holy Spirit you have taught the hearts of your faithful. In the same Spirit, help us to know what is truly right and always to rejoice in your consolation.

We ask this through Christ, Our Lord.

Amen.

A journey of a thousand miles begins with a single step.

Write a prayer to God, reflecting on where you are in your faith journey. Think about your feelings, questions, hopes, and desires. Then begin a conversation with God—your Father and friend.

I, _____, *about to begin my journey to prepare for the Sacrament of Confirmation, offer the following prayer to God.*

_____

_____

_____

_____

_____

_____

_____

_____

_____

Welcome to
CONFIRMED IN THE SPIRIT

ON THE DAY OF YOUR BAPTISM, your parents promised to raise you in the faith and to see that the divine life, which God gives you, is kept safe and grows stronger in your heart. They accepted the responsibility of teaching you what it means to be Catholic and to keep God's commandments, as Jesus taught us, by loving God and your neighbor.

At your Baptism the Holy Spirit filled you with gifts and graces to guide you. Since then, your parents, sponsors, parish priest, catechists, and other good Christians have helped you live the life God has intended for you. Through the celebration of the Eucharist, you have strengthened yourself to respond to God's calling. You also have had to be reconciled with God and your neighbor through the Sacrament of Penance and Reconciliation. Now you are getting ready to take another step—celebrating the Sacrament of Confirmation.

Confirmed in the Spirit will help you prepare to be strengthened by the Holy Spirit in the Sacrament of Confirmation. You will review many of the truths you have learned, and you will deepen your understanding of how Confirmation is linked to both Baptism and the Eucharist. More importantly, you will consider how the Holy Spirit can help you choose wisely and act responsibly as you learn how to stay attuned to the Spirit's voice and to obey it faithfully.

As you journey deeper into this book, you will gain a greater appreciation for what it means to be confirmed in the Spirit. You will come to realize that only the Spirit of Jesus can help you give witness to the Gospel and serve the Kingdom of God. Two thousand years ago, Saint Paul wrote about the goals of all Christians and the challenges they face. He spoke about God's call and promise. "Now the one who has prepared us for this very thing is God, who has given us the Spirit as a first installment." (2 Corinthians 5:5)

CHAPTER 1

Confirmed in the Spirit

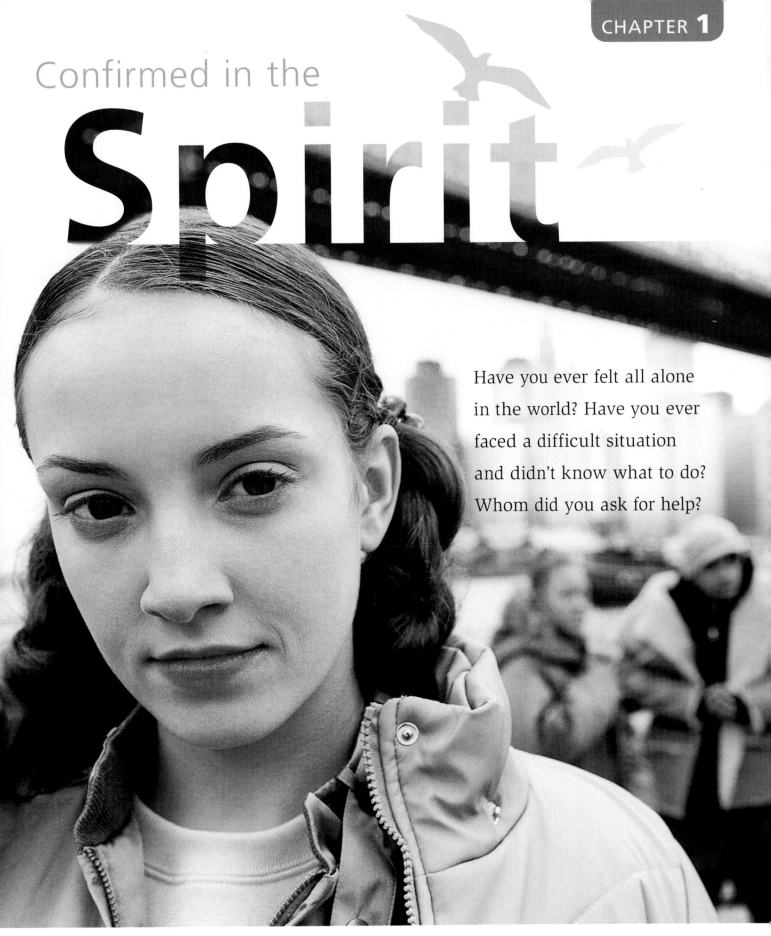

Have you ever felt all alone in the world? Have you ever faced a difficult situation and didn't know what to do? Whom did you ask for help?

"Let us pray to our Father that he will pour out the Holy Spirit to strengthen his sons and daughters with his gifts . . ." *—Rite of Confirmation*

The Spirit Is with Us

"If you love me, you will keep my commandments. And I will ask the Father, and he will give you another Advocate to be with you always, the Spirit of truth, which the world cannot accept, because it neither sees nor knows it. But you know it, because it remains with you, and will be in you. I will not leave you orphans."

John 14:15–18

Understanding Scripture

In the passage above, Jesus is talking to his Apostles after the Last Supper. He is giving them some final words of comfort before his accusers come to arrest him. The Apostles are nervous, and they're wondering what's coming next. Jesus doesn't deny that he is leaving.

The disciples are afraid of being left behind; they will be lost without Jesus. But Jesus tells them he is sending an **Advocate** to help them.

The term *advocate* comes from a Greek word that can mean "lawyer." It can also mean "mediator," "intercessor," "comforter," or "consoler."

Jesus calls on the "Spirit of Truth" to be his friends' advocate and remain with them. Jesus offers us the same support. He tells us, "I will not leave you orphans." (John 14:18)

Scripture and You

Facing the challenges of a new day can be scary. You may have to deal with a difficult situation at home or at school. You may be disturbed by the events you see unfolding in the world. With so many problems facing the world and yourself, you may wonder where God is.

You are just like the disciples listening to Jesus. They have been with him for almost three years, and now he is leaving them. They're trying to make sense of what's happening and are wondering what will come next.

Jesus assures the disciples that he won't leave them orphans. He promises to send God the Holy Spirit, the Third Person of the Trinity to be with them always. Jesus makes that same promise to you today.

REFLECTING ON GOD'S WORD

What comes to mind when you hear Jesus promise not to leave you as an orphan? What problems or concerns can you ask the Holy Spirit to help you handle? Spend a few moments in prayer. Silently talk to God about anything you would like.

HOLY BIBLE

The Spirit in the Old Testament

Many people think that God really isn't involved in the world; he simply lets things happen. Some see God as a watchmaker who winds up the world and then steps aside and lets it tick away. The Bible tells a completely different story. It says that from the beginning of creation, the Spirit of God formed the earth and all its surroundings, and that God will always be with us.

In the Old Testament, the word for "spirit" is the Hebrew word *ruah,* which can be translated as "wind" or "breath." God's action in creation is described in the Book of Genesis: God created the heavens and the earth. The earth was a shapeless wasteland, and the heavens were covered with darkness. A mighty wind swept across the waters. (Genesis 1:1–2) God formed the first man out of the clay of the ground and breathed into him the Spirit of Life. (Genesis 2:7)

The Spirit of God is with his people throughout the Old Testament. With the help of God's Spirit, Moses leads the Hebrew people out of Egypt to freedom. As the Hebrew community grows, God gives his Spirit to the community's leaders. (Numbers 11:17,25)

The Spirit in the New Testament

In the New Testament, the Holy Spirit comes to Mary as she answers the call to be the mother of Jesus, the Son of God. (Luke 1:35) The Holy Spirit appears in the form of a dove at Jesus' baptism. (Matthew 3:16–17) Jesus is led by the Spirit into the desert to pray. (Luke 4:1–2) And Jesus reads from the scroll of the prophet Isaiah

Annunciation, He Qi, 2001.

that the Spirit is upon him as he begins his ministry. (Luke 4:16–21)

After Jesus' Resurrection and Ascension, the Holy Spirit comes on Pentecost. The Spirit fills the disciples with grace and gives them the courage to proclaim Jesus to the world. (Acts of the Apostles 2:1–4)

The Spirit in the World Today

The gift of God that helps us live as he wants us to live is called **grace.** The Sacrament of Confirmation completes the grace we receive in Baptism. It seals, or confirms, this grace through the seven Gifts of the Holy Spirit.

The Scripture stories of the Holy Spirit in action exemplify what God has done in the past, and they are also models of how God continues to work in our lives today. The stories help us recognize the work of the Holy Spirit in our own lives. The Spirit helps us understand what God is calling us to do. The mission of the Holy Spirit and Jesus are inseparable. Whenever God sends his Son, he always sends his Spirit.

Father, Son, and Spirit with Us

God is not distant from us. He wants us to know how close he is to us. As Jesus said, we are not being left as orphans.

God is our Father, who created the universe from nothing in order to express his love for us. Jesus, God the Son, came to us as Savior and Redeemer to reunite us with God and to restore the relationship we broke by our sin. Jesus is the visible image of the invisible God. But it is the Holy Spirit who reveals Jesus to us. The Holy Spirit is God alive in the world. God the Holy Spirit helps us know we are loved and shows us how to love others.

Jesus sent the Holy Spirit to help, defend, and comfort us. As the Spirit of Truth, the Holy Spirit makes the saving work of Christ present and active in the Church. The Spirit gives us the grace to act for God and others as Jesus did. Using your talents and resources to help others and the world is called **stewardship**.

The Holy Spirit also helps us become part of a community, called the **Church,** or the Body of Christ. Christ fills the members of this community with the Holy Spirit and builds them, animates them, and sends them out to share the Good News with the world.

MY TURN   The Spirit at Work

1. How do you see the Spirit at work in the world today?

_____

_____

2. What is an example of the Holy Spirit helping you in your life?

_____

_____

3. When have you felt God's grace working through you or someone else?

_____

_____

_____

_____

Saint Frances Cabrini.

Spirit-Filled People

The Spirit's presence has helped Christians of every century to live like Jesus and to become saints. Read how Saint Frances Cabrini, whose feast day is November 13, felt the Holy Spirit at work in New York City in 1890.

"No!" The bishop sighed and looked at Mother Frances Cabrini. "No, you do not want the property across the river. There is no drinking water."

"But Bishop," pleaded Frances, never known to give up, "the children in the orphanage need fresh air and a place to run. They can't do it in the crowded house on Fifty-Ninth Street."

"Where will you get the money?" the bishop asked impatiently.

"God will take care. Have faith."

The bishop gave in reluctantly. Frances and her sisters prayed to the Holy Spirit. They begged from butchers, bakers, rich friends, and merchants. Eventually they got the money, food, and clothing they needed. After the orphanage was moved to the newly purchased property, the land was surveyed and a well was found.

With the guidance of the Spirit, Frances Cabrini was able to help build nearly 70 institutions for those who were poor and suffering. She crossed the ocean 30 times to help people in need, proving that nothing stops a Spirit-filled Catholic. Saints are ordinary Catholics. They rely on the Holy Spirit and follow wherever he leads them.

Your Christian Name

At your Baptism you were given your Christian name. You may have been named after a relative or a saint or some other person your parents thought would be a good role model for you. As you seal your Baptism in Confirmation, you can keep that name or choose the name of another saint or holy person to be your model of Christian life.

MY TURN   Called to Service

The Spirit gives you the strength to help your neighbors just as he did for Saint Frances Cabrini. Write how you could help a person or group in need.

_____

_____

_____

_____

_____

_____

_____

_____

_____

_____

_____

_____

Images of the Spirit

To help us understand the Holy Spirit, the *Catechism of the Catholic Church* presents a number of images of him. Reflecting on some of these images helps us think about the Holy Spirit in different ways and consider what he means to our lives.

Water

Water signifies regeneration and renewal by the Holy Spirit in Baptism, which is necessary for Salvation. In the Holy Spirit, we are baptized into new life in Christ and become children of God the Father. (Acts of the Apostles 11:16)

Anointing

Anointing with oil has become so identified with the Holy Spirit that it is almost a synonym for the coming of the Spirit. Messiah is the Hebrew word for "anointed one." Christ is from the Greek and also means "anointed one." Jesus is the Messiah, the one uniquely "anointed" by the Spirit. It is a symbol of the Holy Spirit's uniting us with Jesus, the Messiah, the Anointed One. (Acts of the Apostles 10:38; 1 John 2:20–27) Jesus pours out this same Spirit upon us, calling us to be more than we can ever hope to be through our efforts alone.

Rite

We listen to the Scriptures, the inspired Word of God. They tell us about the Father's love for us, who sent his own Son, Jesus Christ, the Word of God made flesh, to save us.

Meaning

Every time you listen to Scripture, inspired by the Holy Spirit, God speaks to you.

Daily Life

The Holy Spirit guides us and gives us strength throughout the day, inspiring all the good that we do.

Life of Faith

Strengthened by the Holy Spirit, we are called to proclaim the Word of the Lord in word and action.

symbol

Fire

Fire symbolizes the transforming energy of the Holy Spirit. John the Baptist proclaimed that Jesus was the one who would baptize with the Holy Spirit and with fire. We also remember the dramatic events of Pentecost in which tongues "as of fire" rested on the disciples. (Acts of the Apostles 2:3)

Dove

Think of a dove, a gentle bird, flying to your hand and gently resting on it. In a similar way, the Holy Spirit rested on Jesus when he emerged from the waters of his baptism by John. He also gently rests on us and remains with us. (Matthew 3:16)

Wind

The Holy Spirit is also represented by wind. We cannot see the wind, but we can feel it. Much like God, we can see how the wind affects everyone and everything it touches. The "strong driving wind" that appeared on Pentecost was reminiscent of the wind that blew over the waters at the beginning of creation. (Genesis 1:2) The wind calls attention to the Holy Spirit breathing life into the Church. (Acts of the Apostles 2:2)

MY TURN | Your Image of the Spirit

1. **Based on what you know about the Holy Spirit, which symbol of the Holy Spirit best relates to your life? Why?**

_____

_____

_____

_____

2. **What is another object, element, or animal that could be a symbol of the Holy Spirit? For you, what is the symbolism?**

_____

_____

_____

A Confirmed Commitment

You are preparing to receive a special outpouring of the Holy Spirit in the Sacrament of Confirmation, an opportunity to deepen your commitment to Jesus and his Church. The grace of the Holy Spirit unites us by faith and by our Baptism to the Passion, Death, Resurrection, and Ascension of Christ. In Confirmation the Holy Spirit brings us closer to Christ, brings us into a closer relationship with the Church, and helps us be a witness to our faith in what we say and do. You've heard the phrase "Practice what you preach." Confirmation gives us the strength to live out and act on our beliefs.

The Spirit Helper

No matter how uncertain you may feel and however many questions you might have, the Spirit is always ready to help you. In Confirmation he comes to you in a special way. This gift of the Holy Spirit in Confirmation will help you explore the many questions in your life and will help you live the life to which God calls you.

Consider the following questions. Choose one and write about it in your journal. Then write a short prayer to the Holy Spirit for guidance. Your journal will not be turned in and no one else will read it.

- How can I plan to be a better person?

- How can I make good choices?

- How do I prepare for the future when I don't understand what's happening today?

Gospel Writer: Saint John the Evangelist

Saint John the Evangelist had the experience of living with Jesus—walking at his side, watching him perform miracles, listening to his teaching, and receiving signs of Jesus' love. John had the special privilege of being with Jesus at crucial times, and he heard Jesus' promise to send the Holy Spirit. After Jesus had sent the Holy Spirit upon the Apostles, John continued to respond to Jesus' call through his writing and preaching.

John was inspired by the Holy Spirit to write his Gospel. The symbol for John as a Gospel writer is the eagle. Tradition holds that he is also the author of the three letters of John and the Book of Revelation in the New Testament. Each time John preached, he emphasized the same message: "Little children, love one another." He said that this is the Lord's Word, and if people followed this message, they would do enough. John was exiled to the isle of Patmos, where he later died. Saint John the Evangelist's feast day is December 27.

2   ACT

Introduction to Catholic Social Teaching Themes

Through the Gospels we learn that Jesus wants us to care for those in need. The social teachings of the Church call us to follow Jesus' example. These teachings are about how to build a just society and live holy lives amid the challenges of the modern world. The bishops of the United States have defined seven areas of social concern for today's Church:

Life and Dignity of the Human Person All human life is sacred, and all people must be respected and valued over material goods.

Call to Family, Community, and Participation Participation in family and community is central to our faith and a healthy society.

Rights and Responsibilities Every person has a right to life as well as a right to those things required for human decency.

Option for the Poor and Vulnerable We are called to pay special attention to the needs of those who are poor and vulnerable by defending and promoting their dignity and by meeting their immediate material needs.

The Dignity of Work and the Rights of Workers The basic rights of workers must be respected. The economy is meant to serve people; work is not merely a way to make a living but an important way in which we participate in God's creation.

Solidarity Since God is our Father, we are all brothers and sisters with the responsibility to care for one another.

Care for God's Creation God is the creator of all people and all things. The responsibility to care for all that God has made is a requirement of our faith.

3   PRAY

Call to Prayer

Saint Augustine observed: "You have made us, O God, for yourself, and our hearts shall find no rest until they rest in you." Does your heart rest in God? How do you see the Holy Spirit working in your life? How is the Holy Spirit calling you to use your gifts to help others?

pray

Prayer to the Holy Spirit

All: In the name of the Father, and of the Son, and of the Holy Spirit. Amen.

Leader: Gathered as a community of believers, let us listen to God, speaking to us in his Word, today and always.

"If you love me, you will keep my commandments. And I will ask the Father, and he will give you another Advocate to be with you always, the Spirit of truth, which the world cannot accept, because it neither sees nor knows it. But you know it, because it remains with you, and will be in you. I will not leave you orphans."

John 14:15–18

Leader: God sends us the Advocate to help guide us. The Holy Spirit is always present to help us in our faith. With faith-filled hearts, let us pray and reflect.

All: Come, Holy Spirit, fill the hearts of your faithful. And kindle in them the fire of your love. Send forth your Spirit and they shall be created. And you shall renew the face of the earth.

Leader: Together we pray to the Holy Spirit for guidance and grace.

All: O God, by the light of the Holy Spirit you have taught the hearts of your faithful. In the same Spirit, help us to know what is truly right and always to rejoice in your consolation. We ask this through Christ, Our Lord. Amen.

Leader: In the Sacrament of Confirmation, the Spirit is with us in a special way. The Spirit renews the face of the earth and renews us in Confirmation.

All: Loving God, you continue to nourish our souls. Thank you for sending the Holy Spirit to strengthen our faith-filled hearts. Amen.

summary

FAITH SUMMARY

Sent by Jesus, the Holy Spirit comes to us at Baptism and Confirmation. The Spirit gives us the ability to live a Christian life.

REMEMBER

Who is the Holy Spirit?

The Holy Spirit is the Advocate whom Jesus sent to be with us always.

What does the Holy Spirit do?

The Holy Spirit helps us learn what Jesus means to us and gives us the grace to act as Jesus did.

How does the Holy Spirit give meaning to our lives?

The Holy Spirit helps us know we are loved and shows us how to love others.

MY CONFIRMATION JOURNAL

Use your journal to enter more deeply into your preparation for Confirmation. Your journal will not be turned in and no one else will read it. Be sure to complete pages ii–viii at the beginning of your journal. Review your journal periodically to better appreciate and understand God's grace at work in your life as you prepare for Confirmation.

Quietly spend time reflecting and recording on journal pages 1–10.

Words to Know

Advocate	grace
Christ	Messiah
Church	stewardship

REACH OUT

1. Consider your personal mission. Write what you feel called to do as a witness to Christ and his Church. What is your special service? Whom are you called to help? You might also draw a picture of yourself carrying out your mission.

2. The Old Testament word *ruah* can be translated as "wind" or "breath." Just like our breath, the Spirit flows through us and through all parts of life. Reflect on times when you have felt this presence of the Spirit and name three times you have passed his love on to others.

WITH MY SPONSOR

Arrange with your sponsor to share your insights, questions, and ideas from this chapter and how they relate to your conversations from the *Faith to Faith* magazine.

Loving God, help me in my faith and guide me in all that I do. Nourish my soul and strengthen my faith-filled heart. Amen.

review

CONFIRMING THE FACTS

Complete the sentences. If you answer them correctly, the boxed letters will spell confirmed.

1. The disciples of Jesus were filled with the Spirit on _ _ _ _ _ ▪ _ _ _.

2. The Holy Spirit gave the disciples _ ▪ _ _ _ _ _ to proclaim Jesus.

3. The Old Testament word for *spirit* can be translated as "_ _ ▪ _" or "breath."

4. Fire symbolizes the _ _ _ _ _ ▪ _ _ _ _ _ energy of the Spirit.

5. The Holy Spirit rested on Jesus like a dove when Jesus emerged from the waters of his _ _ _ _ ▪ _ _.

6. You receive an _ _ _ _ _ _ ▪ _ _ _ of the Holy Spirit in the Sacrament of Confirmation.

7. For Confirmation you can choose the name of a saint to be your ▪ _ _ _ _ of Christian life.

8. The Spirit _ _ _ _ _ _ _ _ ▪ _ _ our bond with the Church in Confirmation.

9. The Holy Spirit is our _ ▪ _ _ _ _ _ _ _, or defender.

THE SPIRIT OF TRUTH

*Write a **T** for true or **F** for false for the following statements about this chapter. Edit each false answer to make it true.*

_____ 1. The Holy Spirit is referred to as the Spirit of Truth in the Gospel of John.

_____ 2. John the Baptist was the advocate whom Jesus promised to send to help the Apostles.

_____ 3. *Advocate* can mean "mediator," "intercessor," "comforter," or "consoler."

_____ 4. Jesus promised not to leave the disciples as martyrs.

_____ 5. *Messiah* is the Hebrew word meaning "Son of God."

CONFIRMATION PUZZLER

Cross out the first letter and every other letter after. The remaining letters spell four words that tell what the Spirit is for you. List them.

J	H	E	E	S	L	U	P	S	E
C	R	H	C	R	O	I	N	Y	S
K	O	B	L	N	E	W	R	A	C
Q	O	A	M	P	F	J	O	U	R
B	T	X	E	E	R	K	I	I	N
C	T	V	E	Y	R	D	C	F	E
W	S	U	S	P	O	Z	R		

_____

_____

_____

_____

CHAPTER 2

Confirmed in
discipleship

Do you sometimes feel that you don't belong or that you don't fit in with a particular group? Are you looking for a place where you can be yourself? What would that place be like? Who would be there with you?

"We ask you Father, with your Son to send the Holy Spirit upon the water of this font. May all who are buried with Christ in the death of baptism rise also with him to newness of life."

—Rite of Baptism

Gathered Together as God's People

"I will take you away from among the nations, gather you from all the lands, and bring you back to your own soil. I will sprinkle clean water over you to make you clean; from all your impurities and from all your idols I will cleanse you. I will give you a new heart, and a new spirit I will put within you. I will remove the heart of stone from your flesh and give you a heart of flesh. I will put my spirit within you so that you walk in my statutes, observe my ordinances, and keep them. You will live in the land I gave to your ancestors; you will be my people, and I will be your God."

Ezekiel 36:24–28

Understanding Scripture

If you have ever felt homesick, you know how lonely and discouraging it can be. In the Scripture passage above, the prophet Ezekiel writes to the Israelites, who are living far from home and feeling removed from God.

God had promised to take care of the Israelites if they obeyed him. But because they refused to follow his plan, their Temple in Jerusalem was destroyed and they were forced to live in the distant land of Babylon.

Ezekiel is God's messenger to the Israelites. Through him, God promises the Israelites that they will become his people again and return home. He will forgive their sins and fill their hearts with his Spirit so that they become a new people.

Scripture and You

Being born with Original Sin means that we have been born in exile, apart from God. Like the Israelites, we sometimes choose not to obey God. Then we feel far from the place where God wants us to be. We are subject to ignorance, suffering, and death. Ezekiel's words remind us that God keeps his promises and is always ready to bring us back to him. God does this in the Sacraments of Initiation— Baptism, Confirmation, and the Eucharist.

REFLECTING ON GOD'S WORD

Take a moment to rest peacefully in God's presence. Hear his words from the prophet Ezekiel. Of what do you want to be washed clean? What distractions keep you from worshiping God alone? Pray that you will be open to the Holy Spirit, so that your heart may be filled with God's love. Thank God for the Spirit he has given you to help you follow his plan. Take a few moments to listen to God and to speak to him about whatever you would like.

God Calls a People—The Church

God is always inviting us to be part of his family. Like he did with the Israelites, God also made a promise, or covenant, with Abraham and Sarah. He asked them to leave their home and family for a land that he would give them. In return for this sacrifice, God promised that Abraham would become the leader of a great nation of God's people.

Centuries later, God made another covenant. He asked Moses to give his commandments to the Israelites at Mount Sinai. There the Israelites promised to obey God's commandments, and in return, he promised to care for them and be their God.

God has made a new covenant with us through Jesus, his Son. At the Last Supper, Jesus took a cup of wine and said, "This cup is the new covenant in my blood, which will be shed for you." (Luke 22:20)

By his Death, Resurrection, and Ascension, Jesus formed a new community. This new community, his Church, was made up of people who believed in him, followed his teaching, and kept his commandment of loving God and one another. People who follow Jesus are called **disciples.**

On Pentecost, God the Father and Jesus his Son sent the Holy Spirit to fill the disciples with the Spirit's grace. The disciples then told the Good News of Jesus to everyone present. Though the people came from different places and spoke many different languages, the power of the Holy Spirit allowed them to understand the disciples in their own languages. That day three thousand people were baptized and received the gift of the Holy Spirit. The Church was alive. (Acts of the Apostles 2:1–13,41)

Evensong, Margaret Baird, oil on board, 1972.

A Spirit-Filled Community

Brought to life and animated by the Spirit, the believers were formed into a community with four characteristics.

- **Community**—living and praying together; sharing common bonds

- **Message**—learning from the Apostles; proclaiming the Good News

- **Worship**—praying in the Temple; breaking bread as Jesus did

- **Service**—loving one another; caring for the poor

The Church Blossoms

The Church grew as the word about Jesus spread. People who wanted to belong to the Christian community prepared to enter the Church at the annual celebration of Jesus' Death and Resurrection during the Easter Vigil.

These soon-to-be Christians descended into a pool of water to signify dying with Christ, giving up their old way of life, and being born anew in Christ. They were baptized "In the name of the Father, and of the Son, and of the Holy Spirit." The bishop laid hands on them and anointed them with oil, confirming, strengthening, and perfecting the Holy Spirit's presence in them. Their initiation was completed when they received the Eucharist for the first time.

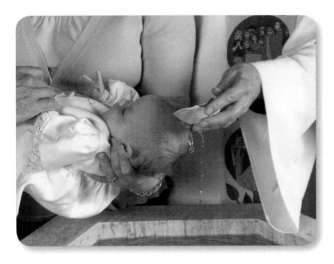

Initiation Today

When a baby is born into a family, it is a special occasion. In the same way, when someone becomes a member of God's family, the Church welcomes him or her through the Sacraments of Initiation: Baptism, Confirmation, and the Eucharist.

In the Eastern Church, Confirmation is celebrated immediately after an infant is baptized and is followed by participation in the Eucharist. Over the course of time, Confirmation and Eucharist became separated from Baptism in the Western Church. Recently the Western Church has emphasized the unity of the Sacraments of Initiation by bringing back the **Rite of Christian Initiation of Adults (RCIA)**. In this rite, adults learn what it means to be a baptized disciple of Jesus—to follow his teachings and to live them every day. Adults are initiated into the Church by celebrating all three sacraments at the Easter Vigil.

MY TURN   Committed to Christ

1. How have you noticed your commitment to God growing as you get older?

_____

_____

_____

_____

2. What is one thing you can do this week to honor and strengthen your commitment to God?

_____

_____

_____

Although your celebrations of Baptism, Confirmation, and Eucharist are probably years apart, they are closely related. First of all, they are sacraments, powerful signs of grace given to the Church by Christ. Divine life, or grace, is given to us through them. The sacraments are the most important signs of God's presence in your life. They help you realize that there is more to life than simply satisfying your own desires. They make present the grace you need to use your time, talent, and energy for the benefit of God and others.

Baptism

We are learning that the Sacraments of Initiation welcome us into the Church. In Baptism, the first sacrament we celebrate, we are freed from Original Sin and born into new life in Jesus.

Baptism is a sign of God's covenant with us. It's an agreement in which God promises to be with us always and to help us build our relationships with him and others. When we accept this covenant, we promise God that we will try to be like Jesus, his model of what it means to be a person for others.

In addition to forming a covenant between God and us, Baptism makes us an adopted son or daughter of God and a member of the Church, the Body of Christ. Baptism marks us permanently as Christians and allows us to share in the priesthood of Jesus, the common priesthood to which all believers belong. United with him in his priesthood, we exhibit the grace of Baptism in all areas of our life—personal, family, social, and as members of the Church—and live out the call to holiness, which is addressed to all the baptized.

The new life we receive in Baptism is called sanctifying grace. This grace takes away Original Sin; it helps us love God, believe in him, and hope in him. It also helps us follow the Holy Spirit, who guides us to live the life God calls us to live.

MY TURN | Being a Disciple

What does it mean to you to be a baptized disciple of Jesus?

_____

_____

_____

_____

_____

_____

_____

_____

Confirmation

You are preparing to celebrate Confirmation, the second Sacrament of Initiation. This time of preparation gives you the opportunity to look carefully at the direction of your life. You need to make decisions every day, and the steady stream of difficult choices can be confusing. This confusion can lead you to question how God is involved in your life or whether he's involved at all.

As we saw in the Scripture passage that began this chapter, God wants to renew us, forgive our sins, and give us hearts full of his Spirit. We will not be alone as we prepare for the difficult decisions of life.

In Confirmation you affirm your baptismal promises. The Sacrament of Confirmation seals your Baptism and reinforces the life-giving gifts you received in Baptism. Confirmation brings you closer to Christ, strengthens the Gifts of the Holy Spirit, unites you more closely to the Church, and helps you follow Jesus' example in your words and actions.

In Confirmation, as in Baptism, you are marked with a permanent character, or seal. Because of this seal, you can only be baptized and confirmed once. Just as you can never stop being someone's brother, sister, or cousin, you can never stop being a child of God once you are baptized.

Eucharist

The Eucharist is the very heart of Catholic life and the greatest prayer we can offer God. This gift from Jesus nourishes and strengthens the community of believers by word and sacrament. At the Eucharist we are most completely the Church. We are God's people, celebrating God's goodness, being redeemed, and sharing God's love. Participation in the Eucharist completes Christian initiation. By receiving it, we continually renew our participation in Christ's saving Passion, Death, Resurrection, and Ascension.

Rite

During the celebration of the Sacrament of Confirmation, you renew your baptismal promises and profess your faith.

Meaning

Confirmation increases and deepens the grace you received at Baptism.

Daily Life

Every time we mirror the life of Christ in our words and deeds, we are living our baptismal promises.

Life of Faith

We recommit to the life of Christ and are strengthened by the grace of the Holy Spirit.

A Closer Look at Confirmation

We all use words and actions to communicate with others. In a similar way, words and actions are signs of what is happening in the sacraments. The signs of Confirmation are the laying on of hands, anointing of the forehead with oil by the bishop, and the words "Be sealed with the Gift of the Holy Spirit."

Anointed with Oil

Just as in Baptism and ordination, oil is used to anoint the newly confirmed. It is called **Chrism**—perfumed oil blessed by the bishop during Holy Week.

Anointing with oil is an ancient ritual that sets someone apart for a special mission. In Israel, priests, prophets, and kings were anointed. As we learned in Chapter 1, both *Christ* and *Messiah* come from words that mean "anointed one."

MY TURN The Laying on of Hands

In the Old Testament, the laying on of hands was a powerful sign of blessing. In the New Testament, hands healed and called down the Spirit. Read the following Scripture passages and write what happens as a result of the laying on of hands.

1. Numbers 27:18–23

_____

2. Luke 4:40

_____

3. Acts of the Apostles 19:4–6

_____

4. 1 Samuel 16:11–13

_____

Centering on Jesus

Are you ready to live your life as a disciple of Jesus? If so, here are some ways you can do it:

- **Pray and celebrate the sacraments.** The Eucharist and the Sacrament of Penance and Reconciliation increase your love for Jesus.

- **Live the Gospel.** Forming habits of Christian living and serving members of your community help you put your faith into action.

- **Study the faith.** You will grow as a faithful Christian through study, reflection, and by sharing your faith with others.

- **Turn to Catholics for support and guidance.** Your parents, sponsors, pastor, catechist, members of your parish, and friends preparing for Confirmation with you will help you prepare to follow Christ together.

Your Sponsor

A **sponsor** will be an important part of your preparation for Confirmation. At your Baptism your parents chose two sponsors for you. Confirmation seals your Baptism. Therefore, you may choose one of your baptismal

sponsors as your Confirmation sponsor, or you may choose another person. Your pastor or catechist will explain to you what is required of your sponsor.

Choosing a Sponsor

Here's how a classified ad requesting a Confirmation sponsor might read.

> ### CONFIRMATION SPONSOR WANTED
>
> *Sponsor wanted to help Confirmation candidate live his or her baptismal promises. Must be willing to share faith life with candidate, be an example of Christian living, represent the Church by supporting candidate, pray with candidate, challenge him or her to live a Christian life, and present candidate to minister of Confirmation. Must be a practicing Catholic, at least 16 years old, and fully initiated by Baptism, Confirmation, and the Eucharist. Pay: immeasurable.*

This may sound like a job few people could fulfill. But you will eventually find a worthy sponsor through prayer, careful thought, and conversations with your parents or other significant adults in your life.

Your sponsor will be someone who will walk with you and offer you guidance as you prepare for Confirmation. On your day of Confirmation, he or she will literally stand behind you and confidently present you to the bishop as a person ready to be sealed with the Gift of the Holy Spirit.

Read the ad with your parents and talk with them who would be a good sponsor for you. Pray to the Holy Spirit for guidance and then discuss the responsibilities with the person you have selected.

1 WITNESS

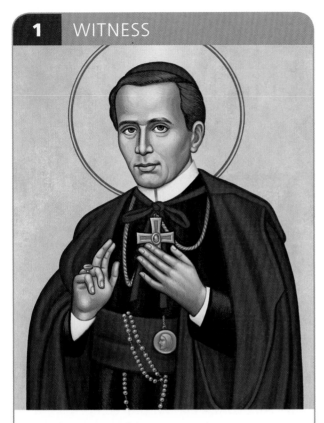

Bishop and Everyman: Saint John Neumann

John Neumann (1811–1860), fourth bishop of Philadelphia, was the first American bishop to be declared a saint. Born in the present-day Czech Republic, he came to the United States in 1835 and was ordained in 1836. In 1852 Neumann was appointed bishop of Philadelphia at a very difficult time. An anti-Catholic political party was setting fire to Catholic schools and convents. Neumann was not deterred by these threats. By 1860 he had established over two hundred Catholic schools. He also established new parishes at the rate of almost one every month. Speaking German, Italian, and English, Neumann was very popular with immigrants, whose dignity as children of God he always respected. People loved hearing the Gospel in their own language. John Neumann was declared a saint in 1977; his feast day is January 5.

2 ACT

Dignity of Human Life

As children of God, we all possess dignity, and we should always treat one another with dignity. God has imprinted his own image and likeness on each of us as human beings and has given us the gift of an incomparable dignity. In the Incarnation, God the Son has taken on our humanity by uniting divine nature with human nature in one Person. Because of the Incarnation, the guiding principle of Catholic Social Teaching is the dignity of the human person. The U.S. bishops have insisted that every economic decision and institution must be judged in light of whether it protects or destroys the dignity of the human person.

3 PRAY

Call to Prayer

The Sacraments of Initiation lay the foundation for our lives as Catholics. Through these sacraments we become full members of the Church. Ask God to be with you and guide you on your journey toward Confirmation.

pray

Grace-Filled Prayer

All: In the name of the Father, and of the Son, and of the Holy Spirit. Amen.

Leader: We have learned about the three Sacraments of Initiation: Baptism, Confirmation, and Eucharist. Now, gathered as a community of believers, let us listen to God, speaking to us in his Word today and always.

"I will take you away from among the nations, gather you from all the lands, and bring you back to your own soil. I will sprinkle clean water over you to make you clean; from all your impurities and from all your idols I will cleanse you. I will give you a new heart, and a new spirit I will put within you. I will remove the heart of stone from your flesh and give you a heart of flesh. I will put my spirit within you so that you walk in my statutes, observe my ordinances, and keep them. You will live in the land I gave to your ancestors; you will be my people, and I will be your God."

Ezekiel 36:24–28

All: Praise to you, Lord Jesus Christ.

Leader: Now let us offer our prayers to God, who offers us new life. That all of us who have been brought to new life in Baptism may always give thanks to God for his life in us.

All: Lord, hear our prayer.

Leader: That as we prepare to celebrate our Confirmation, we may grow in understanding and living our faith.

All: Lord, hear our prayer.

Leader: That our participation in the Eucharist may nourish the new life we received in Baptism.

All: Lord, hear our prayer.

Leader: As Catholics we believe that being born again is the transforming grace we received in Baptism. This grace is with us throughout our lives, helping us turn away from sin and toward God. For this let us give thanks to God.

All: Loving God, through the Sacraments of Initiation, we are given new life in your grace. Thank you for giving us the grace to deepen our relationship with you. Amen.

summary

Words to Know

Chrism
disciple
Original Sin
Rite of Christian
  Initiation of
  Adults (RCIA)

sacrament
sanctifying grace
sponsor

FAITH SUMMARY

Through the Sacraments of Initiation, we become members of the Church who continue the mission of the Church.

REMEMBER

What are the Sacraments of Initiation?

The Sacraments of Initiation are Baptism, Confirmation, and the Eucharist. We are born in Baptism, strengthened in Confirmation, and nourished by the Eucharist.

What are the effects of Baptism?

Baptism is necessary for Salvation. It is our birth into new life in Christ. It frees us from Original Sin and gives us new life in Jesus. It forms a covenant between God and us, in which God promises to be with us always and to help us grow in faith. Baptism gives us sanctifying grace—new life that helps us love God and hope in him.

What does Confirmation do for us?

Confirmation seals our Baptism and deepens baptismal grace. It unites us more firmly to Christ, strengthens the Gifts of the Holy Spirit, brings us closer to the Church, and encourages us to witness to Christ in all circumstances in word and action.

What are four characteristics of the faith community formed by the Holy Spirit?

Four characteristics of the faith community are community, message, worship, and service.

MY CONFIRMATION JOURNAL

Use your journal to enter more deeply into this chapter. Quietly spend time reflecting and recording on journal pages 11–20.

REACH OUT

1. The words of the anointing are based on the practice of stamping something for identification. In the past, letters and documents were sealed with hot wax. A person's seal was pressed into the wax, leaving an imprint. In Confirmation, God marks you as his own. You are called to receive God's mark and authorized to act as his disciple. Draw what God's seal might look like. Then write a description of it.

2. Research your parish community and write about it. Explain how it was founded and how it got its name. Describe how large the parish is, the variety of people who belong to it, and its major activities.

WITH MY SPONSOR

Arrange with your sponsor to share your insights, questions, and ideas from this chapter and how they relate to your conversations from the *Faith to Faith* magazine.

Loving God, thank you for the grace to follow you and the strength to turn away from sin. Amen.

review

WITNESS, PAST AND PRESENT

Read the passages below from the Acts of the Apostles, and write the letter of the characteristic of the Church lived by these early Christians. There may be more than one.

a. message   **c.** worship
b. community   **d.** service

_____ **1.** Acts 2:44–45   _____ **4.** Acts 13:14–18

_____ **2.** Acts 4:34–35   _____ **5.** Acts 2:42

_____ **3.** Acts 8:5–8

AN EXCEPTIONAL EVENT

Complete the sentences. If you finish them correctly, the boxed letters will spell an important event involving the Holy Spirit.

1. At the Last __ __ __ __ __ Jesus formed a new covenant with his blood.

2. By his Death,

__ __ __ __ __ __ __ __ __ __ __ __ , and Ascension, Jesus formed a group of people who followed his teaching and kept his commandment of love.

3. The __ __ __ __ __ __ __ __ __ __ are signs of the Holy Spirit's presence in our lives.

4. __ __ __ __ __ __ __ marks us as Christians.

5. Sanctifying __ __ __ __ __ helps us follow the directions of the Holy Spirit.

6. We promise to try to be like Jesus when we

accept God's __ __ __ __ __ __ __ __ .

7. The Sacrament of

__ __ __ __ __ __ __ __ __ __ __ __ strengthens the gifts we receive in Baptism.

8. __ __ __ __ __ __ is the oil used in Baptism and Confirmation.

9. __ __ __ __ __ __ __ __ __ the faith will help you grow closer to God.

What is the event? _____

EZEKIEL PUZZLER

Complete the crossword puzzle about the Scripture passage you read from the Book of Ezekiel.

Across
5. similar to laws or rules
6. pumps life to the body

Down
1. a cleansing liquid
2. another word for *lands*
3. to make clean
4. received with a new heart

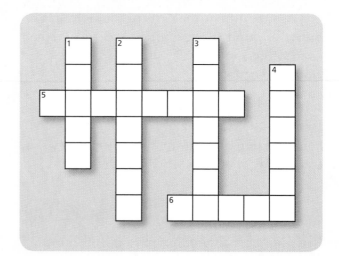

CHAPTER 3

Confirmed in
faith

Think about different groups to which you belong. They may be clubs, sports teams, or your group of friends. What helps you feel like a part of the group? What do these groups have in common?

"This is our faith. This is the faith of the Church. We are proud to profess it in Christ Jesus our Lord." —Rite of Confirmation

Words to Take to Heart

"This then is the commandment, the statutes and the ordinances, which the Lord, your God, has commanded that you be taught to observe in the land you are about to cross into to possess . . . Hear then, Israel, and be careful to observe them, that it may go well with you and that you may increase greatly; for the Lord, the God of your ancestors, promised you a land flowing with milk and honey.

Hear, O Israel! The Lord is our God, the Lord alone! Therefore, you shall love the Lord, your God, with your whole heart, and with your whole being, and with your whole strength. Take to heart these words which I command you today. Keep repeating them to your children. Recite them when you are at home and when you are away, when you lie down and when you get up."

Deuteronomy 6:1,3–7

Understanding Scripture

The first five books of the Old Testament—Genesis, Exodus, Leviticus, Numbers, and Deuteronomy—form the Pentateuch. In Hebrew they are referred to as the Torah, meaning "instruction" or "law." In the Book of Deuteronomy, Moses gives a number of speeches to remind the Israelites that they belong to God.

In Chapter 5 of Deuteronomy, Moses restates the Ten Commandments and reminds the Israelites of all the other laws they have agreed to follow.

In the Scripture passage above, Moses explains that the true way to follow God's instruction is to love God with all your heart, all your soul, and all your strength. Moses stresses that the Israelites should not only know the words of this instruction but that they should also take the instruction to heart, teach it to their children, and use it to guide all their actions.

Scripture and You

During this time of preparation for Confirmation, you will review important aspects of the instruction you have received. The reading from Deuteronomy reminds you to take this instruction to heart.

REFLECTING ON GOD'S WORD

Relax and prepare to spend some quiet time with God. Imagine that you are with the Israelites, listening to Moses's words. God is asking you to love him with all your heart, soul, and strength. Let his words sink in. Ask God to help you make this Confirmation preparation a time to learn more fully what it means to love him above all things.

We Believe

Just as we make a statement with the clothes we wear and the music we listen to, we make a statement by praying and living the Creed. We are stepping out into the world, telling everyone that we are Catholic and identifying ourselves as believers.

Our faith is our personal commitment to God. It involves the assent of our mind and will to God, who has revealed himself in words and action throughout history. We all need the support of our community to help us grow in our faith, a faith that has been handed down to us. During our years of instruction, we've relied on others to help us understand what the Creed means to us. In fact, the words we say in the Nicene Creed go all the way back to the fourth and fifth centuries. The word *creed* comes from the Latin word *credo*, which means "I believe."

The Holy Trinity

The Holy Trinity is at the center of what we believe. We believe in one God who is Father, Son, and Holy Spirit. We follow Jesus, God the Son, because God the Father calls us and God the Holy Spirit moves us.

A Loving Father

Just as the Persons of the Trinity are one in what they are, they are one in what they do. God the Father is credited in a special way with the work of creation. We believe that he is the Creator of everything that exists. People often wonder "Where do we come from?" and "Where are we going?" There is one answer: God the Father.

God the Father created us out of love and to share in his goodness. He created the entire universe by his own wisdom. But he is not an impersonal force; he is present and active in

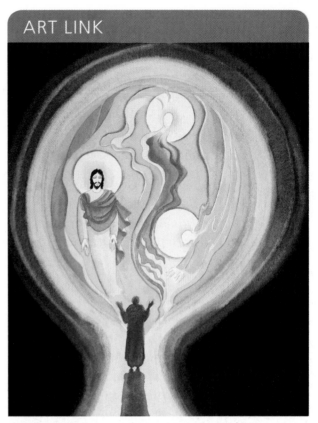

ART LINK

Elizabeth Wang, *Jesus our High Priest, through the Holy Spirit, draws us into the Father's love,* 2010.

our lives. It is Jesus who teaches us to call God "Abba"—Father.

God walks with us to help us achieve the goals he intended for us: eternal happiness with him, sharing his truth, goodness, and beauty.

Our journey begins with Baptism, which frees us from Original Sin. Adam and Eve's act of disobeying God resulted in Original Sin. This sin damaged their relationship with God and caused all humans to be born with Original Sin.

God our Father wishes to bring us from the state of Original Sin to the state of grace. He wants us, as his adopted children, to experience the intimacy of the life of the Trinity and once again share in his holiness. So God sent his Son, Jesus, to be our Savior.

God the Son: Closer to Us

Talking to someone by phone or e-mail is nice, but visiting them in person is even better. To be closer to us, God sent his Son, Jesus, to live among us. When we pray the Creed, we state our belief that the Father sent his only Son, Jesus, to atone for our sins. Jesus is the Word of God, who became human to save us.

Jesus saved us by revealing God's love to us, exemplifying the holiness we should try to achieve, healing our damaged relationship with God, and allowing us to share in his divine nature.

Mary and Jesus, Laura James, 1991.

Fully God, Fully Human

Jesus is fully God and fully human. He became human while remaining truly God. Mary was chosen to be the Mother of God; therefore, her conception was without sin. We celebrate this truth on the Feast of the Immaculate Conception. Jesus was miraculously conceived by the power of the Holy Spirit and born of the Virgin Mary. We are all familiar with the beautiful story of Jesus' birth in Bethlehem.

Jesus lived in Nazareth with Mary, his mother, and Joseph, his foster father, until he was about 30 years old. He then began his life of ministry. Jesus preached about God his Father and the kingdom we are all called to share. For three years Jesus taught people how to live the way God wants us to live. He worked miracles to show the power of the Kingdom of God. Jesus invited sinners into this kingdom.

Envious religious leaders handed Jesus over to Roman officials, claiming that he incited the crowds against Rome. The Romans crucified Jesus. He died and was buried. The Creed states, "For our sake he was crucified . . ." And for our sake, God raised him to new life on the third day.

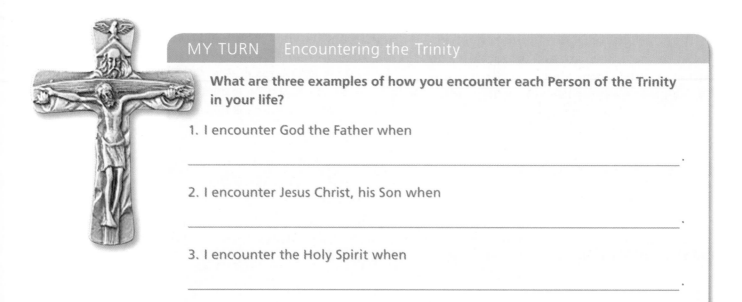

MY TURN Encountering the Trinity

What are three examples of how you encounter each Person of the Trinity in your life?

1. I encounter God the Father when

_____.

2. I encounter Jesus Christ, his Son when

_____.

3. I encounter the Holy Spirit when

_____.

Jesus then appeared to his disciples and later ascended to Heaven to be with God the Father. Our faith assures us that Jesus will come again at the end of time to judge all who have died and those still alive. He will establish God's kingdom of peace and justice forever.

On the night before he died, Jesus shared a meal with his friends. He took bread and wine and transformed them into his Body and Blood. We call this meal the Eucharist. In the Eucharist, Jesus is not only present with us, but the saving events of his life, Death, Resurrection, and Ascension are present as well.

A Sanctifying Spirit

Sometimes we can feel frustrated or lonely. Jesus made sure that we will never be alone. We know that Jesus is with us in the Eucharist. He also sent the Holy Spirit to be with us, help us, and defend us. God the Holy Spirit allows us to experience Jesus' saving presence. In Baptism, we receive through the Holy Spirit the life that God the Father gives us in Jesus, his Son. God the Father, God the Son, and God the Holy Spirit are the Trinity.

The Catholic Church

Another way Jesus made sure we would not be alone was by establishing his Church. The life of the Trinity is lived out in the Church. The Church is a community of pilgrim people on the way to the Father. They are the people whom God gathers in the entire world. They draw their lives from the Word and the Body of Christ and so become Christ's Body, the Church.

The Church is a visible society, governed by the pope and all the bishops, who are the successors of the Apostles. They are called the **Magisterium,** or teaching authority, of the Church. Guided by God the Holy Spirit, they have the authority to preach the gospel and lead the Church. The bishops have the responsibility to proclaim God's message to the people.

MY TURN   United in the Lord

Make a list of Christian beliefs. Use it as a reminder of what all Christians have in common as you pray for unity among all believers in Christ.

_____

_____

_____

_____

_____

_____

_____

When the pope, in union with the bishops, solemnly teaches on a matter of faith and morals, the teaching is called an **infallible** teaching. This means the teaching is free of error.

The Church has four distinguishing marks; the Church is one, holy, catholic, and apostolic.

One

The Church is **one** because it has been made one body in Jesus. Unity is the essence of the Church. All who have been baptized are members of the Church of Christ, whose fullness is found in the Roman Catholic Church. Over time there have been wounds to the Church's unity. The baptized followers of Jesus are no longer united in one Church. As Catholics we are united with Jesus in the desire to see the unity of the Church restored, and we should pray for and work toward that end. This work toward the unity of all Christians is called **ecumenism.**

Holy

The Church is **holy** because Jesus, the Church's founder, is holy. All of the Church's activities are done with the goal of making the entire world a better, holier place. The Church is always in need of purification because all its members are sinners. We are not yet the holy people God calls us to be; we are still on our way to becoming holy.

Catholic

The Church is **catholic,** or open to all, because it has been sent by Christ to the entire human race. Even those who don't believe that Jesus is the Son of God are related to the Church. The Jewish people have already given a positive response to God's call in the Old Testament.

Rite

Your community of faith applauds after you are presented to the bishop.

Meaning

The applause of your community is their way of saying they believe that you are ready to receive the Sacrament of Confirmation.

Daily Life

God speaks to us in many ways. One way is through the people around us.

Life of Faith

When the Church gathers in Jesus' name, he is present. Our community of faith is the Church. We belong to it and share its faith and commitment.

Muslims are included in God's plan of salvation because with us they adore the one, merciful God. Because it is catholic, the Church has a bond with all people through God, who is present in every human heart.

Apostolic

The Church is **apostolic** because the Apostles carried out Jesus' plan of establishing the Church. Today the Apostles' teaching is carried out by their successors, the bishops, in union with the pope.

The mission of the Church and each of its members is Christ's mission—to call all creation into the Kingdom of God. To achieve this goal, the Church teaches the Christian message by word, example, and service to others.

Mosaic of Apostles, Lourdes, France.

| MY TURN | In Other Words |

1. Choose one of the four Marks of the Church, and describe how it is important to the Church.

_____

_____

_____

_____

2. What are some other words that describe the Church? Explain.

_____

_____

_____

_____

Life Everlasting

In Chapter 1 we discussed how a covenant is a promise between God and us. We can choose either to keep or break this promise. In other words, we either accept or reject the grace of God while we're alive. When we die, our time for choosing is over. We will then be judged by God on the good we have done or have failed to do. This is called the **particular judgment.**

People who die in God's grace and friendship and are perfectly purified will live forever with Christ in Heaven. In our families we never forget loved ones who have died. In the same way, the Church includes everyone who has died while believing in Christ and who lived by his example of goodness.

The Communion of Saints is the Church on earth united with all those who have died and are in Heaven or in **Purgatory.** The most esteemed member of the Communion of Saints is Mary, the Mother of God and the Mother of the Church. At the end of her life, Mary's body and soul were taken to Heaven in the **Assumption.** Mary is our example of how the Church will be perfected in Heaven. Those who die in friendship with God, but who still need to be purified of their attachment to sin, experience Purgatory. People who choose to separate themselves completely from God choose a state of exclusion called Hell.

The **Last Judgment** will come when Christ returns in glory and proclaims the end of time as we know it. When Christ comes again, we will know the meaning of God's plan and see how his goodness triumphs over evil. In the end God's love is stronger than death.

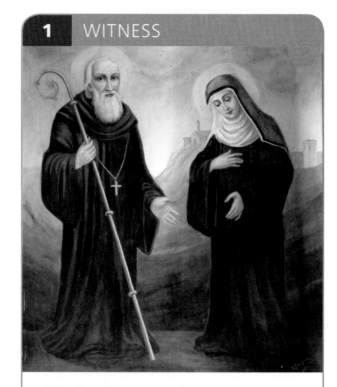

Life in Community: Saint Benedict and Saint Scholastica

There are many ways to serve the Church and make the world a better place. Saints (and siblings) Benedict and Scholastica were born in the 5th century in Norcia, Italy. They founded monasteries and convents where people of faith could dedicate their lives in community to serve God and others. Their motto was *Ora et Labora,* which is Latin for "pray and work." Saint Benedict wrote the *Rule,* a set of guidelines to help his community live as a witness of the Gospel. One of its principles is to be hospitable and welcome others as brothers and sisters, no matter who they are.

There are still many active Benedictine communities throughout the world. They continue to serve others, praying and working in community and giving witness to their faith. Saint Benedict's feast day is July 11, and Saint Scholastica's feast day is February 10.

Call to Family, Community, and Participation

Participation in community—whether in our family, parish, city, or country— is central to our faith and to a healthy society. Families must be supported so that people can participate in society, build a community spirit, and promote the well-being of all, especially those who are poor. How we organize our society—in economics and politics, in law and policy—directly affects human dignity and the capacity of individuals to grow in community. People have a right and a duty to participate in society, seeking together the common good and well-being of all. Our shared faith guides us and gives us principles, values, and counsel on how to promote the family and our participation in the community. The Holy Spirit accompanies and strengthens us so that we might live in the community, the Gospel, and the faith we profess in the Creed.

Our Creed

The Nicene Creed is based on the creed developed at the Council of Nicaea in A.D. 325. At this council the Church bishops defined how Jesus Christ, God the Son, is of the same substance as God the Father and is also fully man. The Creed was given its final form 56 years later in A.D. 381 by the bishops at the Council of Constantinople. At that council the bishops expanded the language about the Holy Spirit. This is the creed held by most Christians. The creed proclaims the perfect unity that exists between the three divine Persons of the Holy Trinity. In response to God's invitation to share in his life, we desire to reflect the unity of the Trinity by striving to be united with one another.

Call to Prayer

Pray the Creed reverently. Be conscious of how your local faith community and all Christians share the beliefs you profess, making us all brothers and sisters in Christ, children of God, who are guided by the Spirit.

faith

Praying the Creed

All: In the name of the Father, and of the Son, and of the Holy Spirit. Amen.

Leader: Gathered as a community of believers, let us listen to God's Word.

"Hear, O Israel! The LORD is our God, the LORD alone! Therefore, you shall love the LORD, your God, with your whole heart, and with your whole being, and with your whole strength. Take to heart these words which I command you today. Keep repeating them to your children. Recite them when you are at home and when you are away, when you lie down and when you get up."

Deuteronomy 6:4–7

Leader: We love God who is Father, Son, and Holy Spirit. Let us pray our Creed, our profession of faith.

All: I believe in one God,
the Father almighty,
maker of heaven and earth,
of all things visible and invisible.

Reader 1: God our Father, you are all-powerful and also my loving Father.

All: I believe in one Lord Jesus Christ, the Only Begotten Son of God, born of the Father before all ages. God from God, Light from Light, true God from true God . . .

Reader 2: How great you are, Lord Jesus. You are God, and you are also man. You are light, and you still know what it is like to be me. You saved me from my sins.

All: I believe in the Holy Spirit, the Lord, the giver of life, who proceeds from the Father and the Son . . .

Reader 3: Holy Spirit, you are always with me. You bring new life through the Sacraments of Initiation, and you reveal Christ to me.

All: I believe in one, holy, catholic and apostolic Church.

Reader 4: May all members of the Church be united in Jesus. Grant that all I do will bring people together.

All: I look forward to the resurrection of the dead and the life of the world to come.

Reader 5: May I one day live forever with you and with those who have died.

All: Amen.

Leader: This is our faith. We are proud to profess it in Christ Jesus our Lord. Let us ask God for his continued assistance and care as we prepare for the Sacrament of Confirmation.

All: Loving God, take us under your tender care, as we prepare for Confirmation. Make us worthy to receive the grace of Confirmation. Help us prepare well for this sacrament which calls us to love, live, and spread the faith. We ask this through Christ our Lord. Amen.

summary

FAITH SUMMARY

God the Holy Spirit helps us believe the Creed, the fundamental truths of our faith, taught by Jesus and his Church.

REMEMBER

What is the statement of our faith?

We profess the Nicene Creed at Mass. It contains the main truths of the Catholic faith.

What is at the center of our faith?

The Trinity is at the center of our faith. We believe in one God, who is Father, Son, and Holy Spirit.

How did God move us from the state of sin to the state of grace?

God sent his Son, Jesus, to be our Savior, to save us from our sins. Jesus repairs our damaged relationship with God, reveals God's love to us, and allows us to share in his divine nature.

What are the four distinguishing Marks of the Church?

The Church is one, holy, catholic, and apostolic.

What is the Communion of Saints?

The Communion of Saints is the Church on earth united with all those who have died and are in Heaven or Purgatory. Mary, the Mother of God and the Church, is the most esteemed member of the Communion of Saints.

When will we fully understand God's plan?

We will understand God's plan at the Last Judgment, when Christ returns in glory and pronounces the end of time as we know it.

MY CONFIRMATION JOURNAL

Use your journal to enter more deeply into this chapter. Quietly spend time reflecting and recording on journal pages 21–30.

Words to Know

apostolic	Kingdom of God
Assumption	Last Judgment
catholic	Magisterium
ecumenism	Nicene Creed
holy	one
Holy Trinity	particular
Immaculate	judgment
Conception	Purgatory
infallible	Torah

REACH OUT

1. Design a bumper sticker depicting a name for God, such as Abba, Father, Creator, Good Shepherd, or another name.

2. Write, produce, and star in a 30-second commercial that teaches a truth of the faith or persuades others to follow Christ. Work on your own or in a small group. Use costumes and props to help get your point across. Videotape your final product.

WITH MY SPONSOR

Arrange with your sponsor to share your insights, questions, and ideas from this chapter and how they relate to your conversations from the *Faith to Faith* magazine.

Loving God, help me prepare well for the Sacrament of Confirmation, which calls me to love, live, and spread the faith in my community and the world. Amen.

review

MAKE IT TRUE

Cross out the word(s) or letter(s) that makes each sentence false. Then make each sentence true by writing the correct word(s).

1. Catholics believe in three Gods.

2. *Creed* comes from the Latin word *credo,* which means "I am with you."

3. Jesus worked miracles to show the power of God's creation.

4. The Catholic Church is a community of people from all over the United States.

5. The goal of unity for all Christians is called ecclesiasticism.

6. The Church is holy because Peter, the Church's founder, is holy.

7. The Church teaches the Christian message by word only.

8. The Church is catholic, or open only to those who are born into the faith.

9. Mary is equal to all the other members of the Communion of Saints.

10. People who die in God's grace and friendship will live forever with Christ in Purgatory.

TRIOS OF TRUTH

Complete each list of three.

1. Three Persons of the Trinity

   _____

   _____

   _____

2. Three states of being that humans can reach after dying

   _____

   _____

   _____

3. Three distinguishing Marks of the Church

   _____

   _____

   _____

CATHOLIC OR NOT?

*Write a **C** before the beliefs that are held by Catholics.*

_____ 1. Jesus is true God and similar to true human.

_____ 2. God the Father is credited in a special way with the work of creation.

_____ 3. Adam and Eve's offense resulted in Original Sin.

_____ 4. Mary was conceived without sin.

_____ 5. Jesus preached God's Word, but he did not do good works.

_____ 6. After his Resurrection, Jesus never appeared to his disciples.

_____ 7. For about three years, Jesus preached about God his Father and the kingdom we are called to share.

_____ 8. The Church is called the Body of Christ.

CHAPTER 4

Confirmed in love

How many choices do you make each day? How often do you make a really important choice? Where do you turn for help in making those important choices?

"[P]our out, we pray, the gifts of the Holy Spirit across the face of the earth and, with the divine grace that was at work when the Gospel was first proclaimed, fill now once more the hearts of believers." —*Collect, Pentecost Mass*

The Beatitudes

Blessed are the poor in spirit,
    for theirs is the kingdom
of heaven.

Blessed are they who mourn,
    for they will be comforted.

Blessed are the meek,
    for they will inherit the land.

Blessed are they who hunger and
    thirst for righteousness,
    for they will be satisfied.

Blessed are the merciful,
    for they will be shown mercy.

Blessed are the clean of heart,
    for they will see God.

Blessed are the peacemakers,
    for they will be called
children of God.

Blessed are they who are
    persecuted for the sake of
righteousness,
    for theirs is the kingdom
of heaven.

Matthew 5:3–10

Understanding Scripture

Jesus tells us that when we are faced with a difficult choice, we can find help in the **Beatitudes** and the **Ten Commandments.** The Beatitudes begin the Sermon on the Mount, the first of five teaching sections in Matthew's Gospel. In this sermon, Jesus gives his new interpretation of many of the laws in the five books of the Torah, which were given to the people by Moses. Jesus calls his followers to a new way of living that moves beyond the Ten Commandments, the core of the law.

With the Beatitudes, Jesus is offering us a new way of life. If we live according to the Beatitudes, we will begin to experience the Kingdom of God.

Scripture and You

Making moral decisions is never easy. The Ten Commandments give us directions—"Keep the Lord's day holy," "Do not kill," "Do not steal," and others. The Beatitudes are a bit different. They are not so much a description of what we should do; rather, they are examples of whom we should be, not just as individuals, but as members of a community for whom the Kingdom of God is both a promise and a present reality.

God wants us to be happy, and following the Beatitudes will help us find happiness. God made us with the desire for happiness so that we would be drawn to him, the one who can make us completely happy.

Each beatitude begins with the Greek word *makarios,* which can be translated as "happy." However, because the Beatitudes are about the happiness that comes from drawing nearer to the Kingdom of God, "blessed" is the best translation. The happiness we are called to cannot be found in riches, fame, or any human achievement; it can only come from trusting God.

The Ten Commandments and the Sermon on the Mount describe the path that leads to true happiness. Sustained by the Holy Spirit, we walk that path, step by step, in our everyday actions.

REFLECTING ON GOD'S WORD

Relax your body and calm your mind. Think about times you have found it difficult to do what you know you should do. Think about Jesus' words of blessing in the Beatitudes. Ask him for help in your difficult times.

Denial,
**Stevie Taylor,
1999.**

love

Called to Be Free

God created us to be free, and we can only be truly happy if we are free. It is within our power to choose to do or not do what is good. Our freedom means that we take responsibility for our actions. The more we choose to do what is good, the freer we become. But choosing to be happy, choosing to be free, is not always easy. Furthermore, the right choice is not always clear.

There are three requirements for any choice to be a good one. First, what you want to do must be good. Helping a friend, cleaning up around the yard, visiting a sick neighbor—these are all good actions. Second, your intention must be good as well. Doing a chore for a neighbor to avoid babysitting your sister is not an example of choosing good. When the reason why you want to do something is not good, even a kind act is not the right decision.

Finally, the circumstances of the choice must be considered. For example, you promised your parents that you would come straight home after school, but on the way home, your friend twisted his ankle. You walked with him to make sure he got home safely, and you were late arriving home as a result. The circumstances made your decision more difficult. You were called to make a much more mature decision, taking into account the needs of your neighbor. It is not always easy to choose according to your conscience, but that is what growing as a Christian is about.

Conscience: Where We Hear God Speak

How do we know what is a good choice? How do we know our intentions are good? Deep within us is a voice that helps us know right from wrong and then act on that knowledge.

cisions

When we take time to put aside distractions and look inside ourselves, we find our **conscience.** Because we are made in the image of God and are drawn to him, our conscience naturally directs us toward choosing good and avoiding evil.

We can be tempted to choose against our conscience because of Original Sin. The formation of our conscience is a lifelong task. It begins in our family and continues through following the teachings of the Church, the friendships we build, and the choices we make. It is our responsibility to continue to form our conscience as we grow. As you will see in the next chapter, the virtues and Gifts of the Holy Spirit will help us do this.

Actions Speak Louder Than Words

Does the way you behave let people know you are a Catholic? Read the situations and consider whether you ever act in these ways.

- Let someone else be the center of attention.

- Go out of your way to make a new person feel comfortable and welcomed.

- Volunteer even when none of your friends do.

- Avoid spreading rumors.

- Sacrifice your free time to visit someone who is sick.

- Admit when you have done something wrong and apologize.

You know what influence a famous musician, a movie star, or a sports hero can have on your life. You might adopt their style of clothing, their likes and dislikes, and maybe even copy their walk, gestures, or expressions. Jesus Christ is our greatest role model and guide for our lives. He instructed us to keep the Ten Commandments. When asked what was the greatest commandment, he responded: "You shall love the Lord your God with all your heart, with all your soul, with all your mind, and with all your strength. The second is this: You shall love your neighbor as yourself." (Mark 12:30–31) At another time he said: "I give you a new commandment: love one another. As I have loved you, so you also should love one another." (John 13:34)

Christian Love

Loving like Jesus means making room in our hearts for all people—our families, our friends, our parish community, our brothers and sisters in other countries, even people we don't especially like. We can do this by showing the warmth, love, and acceptance of Jesus Christ to those who are poor, sick, strangers, even those who have hurt us. Jesus appreciated the response of love he found in people. He praised positive attitudes, generosity, and service.

MY TURN   Responses of Love

The Gospels tell of Jesus' love. Jesus knew that actions speak louder than words, so he practiced what he preached. His love was so powerful that it inspired others to show love. Read each Gospel verse below. Then underline the correct response of love.

1. Mary, the sister of Martha (Luke 10:38–42)

   kindness   listening   service

2. Martha (Luke 10:38–42)

   serving   healing   listening

3. The centurion (Luke 7:1–10)

   teaching   faith   patience

4. Zacchaeus, the tax collector (Luke 19:1–10)

   listening   repentance   mercy

5. The Good Samaritan (Luke 10:29–37)

   mercy   faith   humility

6. The ten lepers (Luke 17:11–19)

   generosity   preaching   expressing thanks

7. Andrew (John 1:40–42)

   joy   singing   leading a friend to Jesus

8. Joseph of Arimathea (Matthew 27:57–60)

   preaching   patience   sharing possessions

9. The women who followed Jesus (Luke 8:1–3)

   hospitality   patience   trust

10. The man who was blind and begging by the roadside (Luke 18:35–43)

    generosity   teaching   faith

Christ in the House of Martha and Mary,
Jan Vermeer, 1654–1656.

Through the Gospels, we learn that Jesus wants us to love and care for others. It is also just as important that we take care of ourselves. Eating right, exercising, and getting enough sleep are essential. We must also remember not to put ourselves down or get caught up in negative thoughts. Life is a gift from God, and when we treat ourselves and one another with respect, we show our love for God.

Christian Service

At Baptism we received the grace that enables us to love and serve others without counting the cost, to see Christ in others, and to avoid hurting others. Grace makes us eager to reach out to others with concern. It leads us to use our gifts and talents to meet others' needs. Confirmation strengthens the love within us.

We show we have loving hearts when we perform works of mercy. As members of the Christian community, we are actively concerned about those who do not have enough clothing, food, or a good home. We meet their physical needs through the **Corporal Works of Mercy.** These works include feeding the hungry, giving drink to the thirsty, clothing the naked, sheltering the homeless, visiting the sick and imprisoned, and burying the dead. Among all these, giving alms to those who are poor is one of the chief witnesses to fraternal charity. It is also a work of justice, pleasing to God.

Rite

The bishop extends his two hands over all the confirmands. The laying on of hands reflects what the first Apostles did to baptize others in the Holy Spirit.

Meaning

The bishop, with his hands extended, asks God to impart on the confirmands the Gifts of the Holy Spirit.

Daily Life

The Holy Spirit works through us and guides us to do the right thing. When we use the gift of our hands to help and care for others, we are honoring the Spirit within us.

Life of Faith

When we extend our hand in a sign of peace, we remember that together we are members of the one Body of Christ, the Church. The Works of Mercy are a guide to how we can serve the Church by helping others.

We also want to help those who are feeling hurt, discouraged, sick, or confused. We meet the emotional and spiritual needs of people through the **Spiritual Works of Mercy**. These works are instructing, admonishing, counseling, comforting, forgiving, bearing wrongs patiently, and praying for others. The Spirit helps us know what to do in order to come to the aid of our neighbor.

One way to love and serve others through the Works of Mercy is to protect people's basic rights. Everyone has the right to food, clothing, shelter, and fair wages. Everyone has the right to life and freedom. Sometimes we work for justice by giving people what they need. Sometimes justice means speaking up for people, teaching them, and standing up for them. Justice is a matter of love.

Your attitude toward service can teach people how to have a heart for others. Is your attitude toward service positive? Do you look for ways to serve others? Do you consider it a privilege to serve? Followers of Jesus who believe that he loves them will show the same love to others.

When we reach out to others in service with the joy and strength of the Holy Spirit, we find we are the ones who really receive. We receive Christ, who lives in the people we serve.

love

MY TURN | Work of Mercy

Think of an example of Jesus performing a Corporal or Spiritual Work of Mercy. Write it and tell which Work of Mercy it exemplifies. Then write how you can reach out to others in service.

_____

_____

_____

_____

_____

_____

ful

Practicing Christian Service

As Christians, we are called to serve others. Think about how you can volunteer your time and talent for the good of the community. Keep a record of the service you do during your time of preparation for Confirmation. Write about it in your journal regularly. After you have reached out to others in Christian service, reflect on your experience. Remember, you may be asked to share what you have written in your journal, but it will not be turned in, and no one else will read it. You might complete the following statements in your journal:

- I showed Christian love and service by . . .

- I chose to do this because . . .

- By doing this service, I learned that Christian service means . . .

- Doing this service helped me . . .

- Two important events that happened to me while doing this project were . . .

- This experience will help me later in life because it taught me . . .

- I can follow up on this experience by . . .

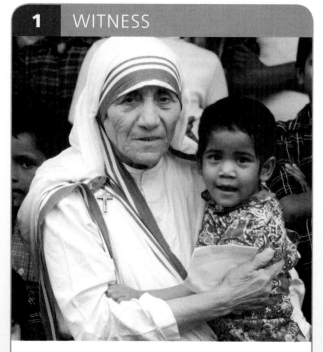

1 WITNESS

Tireless Servant: Blessed Teresa of Calcutta

Blessed Teresa of Calcutta expressed her love for God by working to serve and help those who were less fortunate. She became a nun at age 18 and was then sent to Calcutta, India. When she was 36 years old, she felt a "call within a call." She wanted to help those who were poor and sick and live among them. Sister Teresa decided to dedicate her life to serving the poor and sick, so she moved into the slums of Calcutta. By 1948 she had founded her own order, the Society of the Missionaries of Charity. Mother Teresa established a hospice in Calcutta for those who were destitute and dying. In 1957 the Missionaries of Charity started their work with lepers and the poor in many disaster areas of the world. Mother Teresa received several awards, including the Nobel Peace Prize. She continued to work in Calcutta until her death in 1997. Mother Teresa was beatified in 2003. Her feast day is September 5.

Option for the Poor and Vulnerable

Just as the Holy Spirit called Blessed Teresa of Calcutta, the Spirit of the Lord has been sent to us and calls us to have a special concern for those who are poor. The Kingdom of God is served when we work to assure justice for the poor, release of the oppressed, consolation for the sorrowful, and a new social order in which significant steps are taken so that the needs of people who are poor are addressed. When we receive the Body and Blood of Christ in truth, we will be able to see Christ in our neighbors who suffer most. We are called to see that Jesus' concern for those in need is consistently reflected in our liturgical celebrations.

The Beatitudes

The Beatitudes challenge us to be people of **virtue.** Virtue is a firm attitude, mindset, or disposition to do good. For the virtuous person, doing good is a habit. Whom do you know who is virtuous? How can you model his or her behavior in your own life?

Call to Prayer

The Holy Spirit is already at work within you, drawing you toward God and inspiring your desire to live the Beatitudes as a person of virtue.

pray

Showing Love

All: In the name of the Father, and of the Son, and of the Holy Spirit. Amen.

Leader: Gathered as a community of believers, let us listen to God, speaking to us in his Word today and always.

Leader: Blessed are the poor in spirit,

All: for theirs is the kingdom of heaven.

Leader: Blessed are they who mourn,

All: for they will be comforted.

Leader: Blessed are the meek,

All: for they will inherit the land.

Leader: Blessed are they who hunger and thirst for righteousness,

All: for they will be satisfied.

Leader: Blessed are the merciful,

All: for they will be shown mercy.

Leader: Blessed are the clean of heart,

All: for they will see God.

Leader: Blessed are the peacemakers,

All: for they will be called children of God.

Leader: Blessed are they who are persecuted for the sake of righteousness,

All: for theirs is the kingdom of heaven.

Matthew 5:3–10

Leader: In our preparation for the Sacrament of Confirmation, we learn how our actions demonstrate our love for God. Sometimes we stray from God's love and commit sins. When we recognize our wrongs, we ask for forgiveness. The Beatitudes guide us in the ways we should live.

All: O my God, I love you above all things, with my whole heart and soul, because you are all good and worthy of all my love. I love my neighbor as myself for the love of you. I forgive all who have injured me, and I ask pardon of those whom I have injured. Amen.

Leader: Choosing to do the right thing is choosing to love. In preparation for Confirmation, you are considering ways you express your love of God and your neighbor, your willingness to forgive others, and your desire to be forgiven. Let us thank God for helping us show these acts of love.

All: Loving God, as we prepare for Confirmation, we look to the Beatitudes to support and guide us in our everyday lives. We express our love for you and your Son, Jesus Christ, by acting in faith-filled ways. We thank you for your forgiveness when we stray and ask for the strength to forgive others. Amen.

summary

FAITH SUMMARY

Christians, called to love as Jesus loved, have the Beatitudes and Works of Mercy as guidelines.

REMEMBER

What are the Beatitudes?

The Beatitudes are Jesus' guidelines for Christian living. The Beatitudes include a code of conduct and the promise of happiness in God's kingdom.

What is your conscience?

Conscience is that deepest part of yourself that directs you toward choosing good and avoiding evil.

What is Jesus' new commandment?

"I give you a new commandment: love one another. As I have loved you, so you also should love one another." (John 13:34)

MY CONFIRMATION JOURNAL

Use your journal to enter more deeply into this chapter. Quietly spend time reflecting and recording on journal pages 31–40.

REACH OUT

1. Think about what you have seen on TV or read about in the newspaper lately. Who is in need of justice today? Write about someone in need. Then write what you can do to help.

2. Choose one of the Beatitudes and illustrate it. Then write a description of your illustration.

3. The Beatitudes give us ways to help others. Think about how you can help out at home. You might talk to your parents about it, or you may wish to be a "secret helper." Choose at least one new way you can help. Write about it and keep track of your actions and their outcomes.

Words to Know

Beatitudes	Spiritual Works
conscience	of Mercy
Corporal Works	Ten Commandments
of Mercy	virtue

4. Evaluate how often you reach out in love. For each response of love, rate yourself **1** (not very often), **2** (sometimes), or **3** (often). Think about how you can improve the area where you are most challenged.

_____ Listen

_____ Serve

_____ Forgive

_____ Express thanks

_____ Share

_____ Pray

_____ Welcome

WITH MY SPONSOR

Arrange with your sponsor to share your insights, questions, and ideas from this chapter and how they relate to your conversations from the *Faith to Faith* magazine.

Loving God, guide me in my everyday life to make good decisions and act in faith-filled ways. Thank you for forgiving me when I stray. Give me the strength to do the same for others. Amen.

review

SERVICE WORD SEARCH

Circle the following words in the word search.

Beatitudes   conscience   corporal

kingdom   service   spiritual

F	R	W	X	S	L	C	E	M	E
O	W	C	G	E	C	O	C	R	E
L	C	M	O	D	G	N	I	K	U
B	O	N	S	U	I	S	V	R	Y
E	R	P	N	T	U	C	R	A	J
V	P	O	Y	I	P	I	E	O	M
I	O	Y	S	T	B	E	S	L	Q
P	R	C	V	A	O	N	L	U	X
K	A	J	B	E	W	C	W	C	M
X	L	F	W	B	A	E	C	L	B
I	S	P	I	R	I	T	U	A	L

MAKE IT TRUE

*Write **T** for true and **F** for false. Make each false statement true.*

_____ 1. The Beatitudes begin the Sermon on the Mount.

_____

_____ 2. The core of the law, the Ten Commandments, was given by God to Moses.

_____

_____ 3. The Beatitudes replace the Ten Commandments.

_____

_____ 4. Your intention must be good in order to make a good choice.

_____

CONFIRMATION CROSSWORD

Across

1. directs us toward good

3. called children of God

4. Our conscience helps us make good ones.

6. We are called to provide it.

Down

2. Moses gave us these.

5. Jesus appreciated this in people.

CHAPTER 5

Confirmed in
holiness

What are some of your talents? What are some things you do to improve them? Name some of the ways you are putting your talents to good use.

"Send your Holy Spirit upon them to be their Helper and Guide. Give them the spirit of wisdom and understanding, the spirit of right judgment and courage, the spirit of knowledge and reverence. Fill them with the spirit of wonder and awe in your presence." *—Rite of Confirmation*

Led by the Spirit

For those who are led by the Spirit of God are children of God. For you did not receive a spirit of slavery to fall back into fear, but you received a spirit of adoption, through which we cry, "Abba, Father!" The Spirit itself bears witness with our spirit that we are children of God. . . .

In the same way, the Spirit too comes to the aid of our weakness; for we do not know how to pray as we ought, but the Spirit itself intercedes with inexpressible groanings. And the one who searches hearts knows what is the intention of the Spirit, because it intercedes for the holy ones according to God's will.

We know that all things work for good for those who love God, who are called according to his purpose.

Romans 8:14–16,26–28

Understanding Scripture

Sometimes, trying to put your talents to use is hard work. But Paul's words to the Christians in Rome encourage us. Paul is reminding them that through Jesus' Death, Resurrection, and Ascension, they received the Holy Spirit and have become God's children. All people, Gentiles as well as Jews, can now call God *Abba,* or Father. The people God formed through Abraham now include the Gentiles as well. The Letter to the Romans discusses how the effects of Adam's sin have been reversed in Jesus, the new Adam. It also explains how the sufferings the Gentiles endure are overcome by the hope that they have been given through the "Spirit of adoption."

Scripture and You

All of us excel in certain areas and struggle in others. Because we are adopted children of God, we are able to use our talents in spite of our natural weaknesses. When prayer is difficult for us, the Spirit intercedes, helping us be good, and calling us to be holy. In this chapter we will look more closely at the gifts the Holy Spirit gives to help us.

REFLECTING ON GOD'S WORD

As you quiet yourself to reflect fully on God's Word, be aware of your breath as you slowly breathe in and out. Invite the Holy Spirit to help you with anything in your life with which you may be struggling. Conclude by giving thanks for the Spirit's guidance.

The Theological Virtues

Christopher began taking piano lessons when he was six. His parents saw that he had a real talent for music, so they gave him the chance to develop his gift. Taking time every day was not easy, and he had many disagreements with his parents about whether he practiced enough. But there was something he really enjoyed about making music, so he stuck with it. Now at 14, he's glad he continued playing the piano. There are still times he would rather do anything but practice, but he realizes now that he doesn't have to think too much about the physical part of playing. He can let the skills he has developed lead him and use his heart to make beautiful music.

As children of God, we receive the gift of the **Theological Virtues** of faith, hope, and charity through the Holy Spirit. This gift must also be nurtured and developed. These virtues have their source in God, are infused in us by him, and as we grow in using them, we are drawn more deeply into the mystery of God. That is why they are called "Theological."

Just as practicing the piano helped Christopher develop his gift for music, practicing these virtues strengthens us over time and helps us make good decisions and give the best of ourselves.

Faith

Faith, God's gift to you, is the ability to believe in God and give your life to him. It makes you able to trust God completely and to accept all that he has revealed and teaches through the Catholic Church.

Hope

Hope is closely related to faith. It is the desire for all the good things God has planned for

Lamentation pour Haiti, Tamara Natalie Madden, **United States, 21st century.**

you. Hope gives you confidence that God will always be with you and that you will live with him forever in Heaven.

Charity

Charity leads you to love God above all things and to love your neighbor as yourself. This love involves more than just feelings; it is the way you think and act toward God and others. Charity brings all the virtues together in perfect harmony. Saint Paul writes, "So faith, hope, love remain, these three; but the greatest of these is love." (1 Corinthians 13:13)

As you practice the virtues of faith, hope, and charity and grow in your relationship with God, your ability to practice the Cardinal Virtues also grows.

The Cardinal Virtues

The virtues you acquire by human effort are called **Cardinal Virtues**. *Cardinal* comes from the Latin *cardo*, which means "hinge." All your moral strengths depend on these virtues. They are prudence, justice, fortitude, and temperance. These human virtues are rooted in the Theological Virtues that are given to you by God to help you act as his child.

Prudence

Prudence helps you decide what is good and then choose to do it. It leads you to stop and think before you act.

Justice

Justice leads you to respect the rights of others and to give them what is rightfully theirs. The just person considers the needs of others and always tries to be fair.

Fortitude

Fortitude gives you the courage to do what is right even when it is very difficult. It provides you the strength to resist the temptations you face and, even when it is challenging, to do what you know is right.

Temperance

Temperance helps you balance what you want with what you need. It helps you moderate your desire for enjoyment and builds self-control.

Like playing the piano, being a good friend, playing sports, or anything else worthwhile, these virtues take time and effort to develop. But through practice they can become a natural part of your life. With God's help, the Cardinal Virtues build character and make it easier to do what is right. These virtues will help you achieve your goals and be who God wants you to be.

> **MY TURN** How Virtues Help Us
>
> **Describe a situation in which you displayed one of the virtues. Which virtue did you display, and how did it help you?**
>
> _____
>
> _____
>
> _____
>
> _____
>
> _____
>
> _____
>
> _____
>
> _____

Unwrapping the Gifts of the Spirit

The Cardinal and Theological Virtues are strengths that can improve your life if you practice them. The seven **Gifts of the Holy Spirit,** which you received at Baptism, help you live a life of virtue. These gifts are strengthened in Confirmation. They help you keep your friendship with God strong and guide you in critical situations when you find it hard to cope with problems, difficult situations in life, or making decisions. They help you respond to God fully and lovingly.

Four gifts help you know God's will. The other three help you do his will. Read about each gift of the Spirit and reflect on how he is already at work in your life.

Know God's Will
- wisdom
- understanding
- counsel
- knowledge

Do God's Will
- fortitude
- piety
- fear of the Lord

Wisdom

Just as piano players' music becomes more complicated the longer they play, life becomes more complex the older you get. Everywhere you turn, people are telling you how to act, what to wear, what to believe, who your friends should be, and what music to listen to. How do you know what is best for you?

Wisdom enables you to see life from God's point of view and to recognize the real value of people, events, and things. Wisdom keeps you from foolishly judging only by appearances. It helps you mature in the way you think and act. Wisdom leads you to see the value of being confirmed not because your parents expect it, or because everyone your age is doing it, but because you see its value for you and desire it.

MY TURN | Signs of the Spirit

1. **Titus was a young bishop and a friend of Saint Paul's. Read Titus 3:1–2. What signs of the Spirit is Titus urged to show?**

_____

_____

_____

2. **Write how these signs can help you show loving service.**

_____

_____

_____

Saint Paul.

53

Understanding

When you were younger, you learned that there were things you should and should not do. You learned rules and followed them because you trusted the people who made them, such as your parents. However, you may not have always understood *why* these rules were made. The same might be true with your faith. So how will you be able to really understand your faith and what it means to be Catholic?

Understanding grows through prayer and the reading of Scripture. It gives you insight into the truths of the faith and being a follower of Jesus', and it helps you make right choices in your relationships with God and others.

Counsel

Have you ever agonized over a difficult decision? Did it make you feel confused, hurt, and alone? How did you know what was the right thing to do?

The gift of **counsel,** or right judgment, helps you seek advice and be open to the advice of others. Using this gift, you seek direction in the Sacrament of Reconciliation, and you ask advice from parents or friends. Counsel also helps you give advice. With counsel, you are able to help others with their problems. You speak up and encourage them to do the right thing.

Today, through the gift of counsel, you are determining what being confirmed means in your life. You turn to your parents, sponsor, parish priest, catechists, and others for help in taking this next step in your spiritual journey.

Rite

The bishop anoints your forehead with holy Chrism, or holy oil, as you are confirmed.

Meaning

Oil symbolizes strengthening, healing, cleansing, joy, and consecration. When you are anointed at Confirmation, the Holy Spirit marks your soul with the permanent spiritual seal. This seal unites us more firmly to Christ.

Daily Life

God speaks to us through the gifts and talents he has given us. When we use our gifts to the best of our ability, it is for the betterment of ourselves and others.

Life of Faith

By receiving the Gifts of the Holy Spirit, we have been transformed. We have been marked as Christians. We belong to our parish community as well as to the universal church.

Knowledge

Having an awareness of God's plan will help you live a meaningful life. Knowing Jesus' teachings and taking them to heart will help you be a good Christian. How can you be open to what God has to teach you about life?

The gift of **knowledge** helps you know what God asks of you and how you should respond. You come to know God. You come to know who you are and the real value of things through your experiences. This gift also helps you recognize temptations for what they are and turn to God for help.

The gift of knowledge is at work in you as you contemplate living a Christian life. What you know of Jesus and his example and what you know of the Church—its worship, its beliefs, its teachings, and its call to serve those in need—will help you commit yourself to Christ and the Church as a confirmed Christian.

Fortitude

There is a difference between knowing the right thing to do and actually doing it. You face pressure about using drugs and alcohol. Movies and songs tell you that sex is just about feeling good and that violence is acceptable. Popular culture, and many of the ads with which we are constantly bombarded, would have us believe

Seven Gifts of the Holy Spirit, Eyob Mergia, 2009.

that consumerism and selfishness are widely accepted and encouraged. It's not always cool to speak out about injustices you see around you. How can you find the strength to live by the principles and values of Jesus?

The gift of **fortitude,** or courage, enables you to stand up for your beliefs and to live as a follower of Jesus. With this gift, you have the inner strength to do what is right in the face of difficulties and to endure suffering with faith. Fortitude helps you undertake challenging tasks in the service of your faith. But it also takes fortitude to be faithful to ordinary duties. It takes strength to live a good Christian life even when no one praises you or notices your efforts.

MY TURN   Prayer to the Holy Spirit

1. **Which Gift of the Holy Spirit are you in need of the most? Why?**

_____

_____

2. **Write a prayer to the Holy Spirit, asking for guidance with the gift you chose.**

_____

_____

_____

Piety

It is not uncommon to see people showing little respect for others, for the environment, even for themselves. They destroy things that God has given us to enjoy. This wouldn't happen if people had a sense of God's presence in others and in the world. How can you be more aware of God's presence in your life and in others?

Piety, or reverence, is a gift that helps you love and worship God. It calls you to be faithful in your relationships with God and others. Piety also helps you be respectful and generous.

In the Sacrament of Confirmation, piety helps you strengthen your relationship with God and increase your love for others and the world— for all that God has created.

Fear of the Lord

Out of respect, Moses removed his sandals when God spoke to him from the burning bush. (Exodus 3:1–15) Many Jews today do not pronounce the name of God out of respect. We can learn from their example by honoring God, who is awesome and who loves us.

Fear of the Lord, sometimes called wonder and awe, helps you recognize the greatness of God and your dependence on him. It leads you to marvel at God's incredible love for you.

The gift of fear of the Lord increases your desire to draw closer to God by confirming the great gift you received in Baptism. Awe will inspire you to celebrate the Eucharist. You will experience awe in celebrating the Sacrament of Reconciliation as you recognize God's great love in forgiving you of the sins you've committed.

Right now you are deciding to reflect on your faith seriously. It is difficult to try to change your habits and follow Jesus more completely. It's a challenge to pray more, to participate in the Eucharist more intentionally, to serve others. However, the Gifts of the Holy Spirit, the Theological Virtues, the Cardinal Virtues, and the community of believers who surround you will help and guide you.

Doctor of the Church: Saint Catherine of Siena

The Holy Spirit helps us be good and calls us to holiness. Catherine of Siena heard that call at an early age and decided to devote her life to God. Catherine joined the Third Order of Saint Dominic at age 16. She often locked herself in her room to pray, leaving only to attend Mass. After three years, Jesus spoke to her, saying, "The only way you can serve me, Catherine, is in service of your neighbor." Catherine realized that she had been given gifts with which to serve others. She began to visit prisoners, encouraging them to repent. When a plague came, she took care of the plague-ridden, brought food and clothing, and buried the dead. Her gifts of prophesy and spiritual guidance became widely recognized, and she dictated more than 400 letters and two books. At this time the pope, a Frenchman, lived in Avignon and took orders from the French king. This confused Christians. Catherine went to Avignon and persuaded the pope to return to Rome. In 1970 the Church gave her the special title of Doctor of the Church. Saint Catherine of Siena's feast day is April 29.

Rights and Responsibilities

Saint Catherine of Siena was called to serve the Church. She felt it was her duty and responsibility to use her gifts and offer her life for the good of the Church. We as human beings have both rights and responsibilities. We have intelligence and free will. We have a fundamental right to life and the right to things we need to live such as food, shelter, employment, health care, and education. Along with these rights, we have corresponding responsibilities to respect the rights of all people. Our rights and responsibilities are universal and inviolable. This means that they cannot be taken from us and we cannot give them away. We cannot claim our rights while neglecting our duty to protect these rights for others. The Church teaches that government authority carries serious responsibilities. The chief concern of civil authorities must be to ensure that the rights of individual citizens are acknowledged, respected, defended, and promoted.

Gifts of the Spirit

The Gifts of the Holy Spirit guided Saint Catherine of Siena in her devotion to the Church. Through Jesus, the Gifts of the Holy Spirit that we receive in Baptism are strengthened in the Sacrament of Confirmation. They are wisdom, understanding, counsel, fortitude, knowledge, piety, and fear of the Lord. Which gift do you identify with most?

Call to Prayer

Through the Sacrament of Confirmation, our relationship with God is made stronger. In this way we are equipped to become better witnesses to Christ in the world.

My Lord and Guardian

All: In the name of the Father, and of the Son, and of the Holy Spirit. Amen.

Leader: Gathered as a community of believers, let us listen to God, speaking to us in his Word today and always.

For those who are led by the Spirit of God are children of God. For you did not receive a spirit of slavery to fall back into fear, but you received a spirit of adoption, through which we cry, "Abba, Father!" The Spirit itself bears witness with our spirit that we are children of God. . . .

In the same way, the Spirit too comes to the aid of our weakness; for we do not know how to pray as we ought, but the Spirit itself intercedes with inexpressible groanings. And the one who searches hearts knows what is the intention of the Spirit, because it intercedes for the holy ones according to God's will.

We know that all things work for good for those who love God, who are called according to his purpose.

Romans 8:14–16,26–28

Leader: The Spirit of God comes to our aid, guides us, and blesses us with many gifts. Let us pray together and think about the wonderful gifts from the Lord, who helps and protects us always.

Group A: I raise my eyes toward the mountains. From where will my help come?

Group B: My help comes from the LORD, the maker of heaven and earth.

Group A: God will not allow your foot to slip; your guardian does not sleep.

Group B: Truly, the guardian of Israel never slumbers nor sleeps.

Group A: The LORD is your guardian; the LORD is your shade at your right hand.

Group B: By day the sun cannot harm you, nor the moon by night.

Group A: The LORD will guard you from all evil, will always guard your life.

Group B: The LORD will guard your coming and going both now and forever.

adapted from Psalm 121

Leader: Confirmation is an opportunity to pause and recognize the gifts we have already received and the gifts we will receive from the Holy Spirit, to thank God for them, and to ask for help in using them to serve God and others. Let us join now in praying the Glory Be to the Father.

All: Glory be to the Father, and to the Son, and to the Holy Spirit. As it was in the beginning, is now, and ever shall be, world without end. Amen.

summary

FAITH SUMMARY

The Gifts of the Holy Spirit help us be the people God calls us to be.

REMEMBER

What are the Gifts of the Holy Spirit?

The Gifts of the Holy Spirit are powers given to us at Baptism and strengthened at Confirmation. They help us live virtuous lives, persevere in our friendship with God, and guide us in our decisions and conduct so we become more like Jesus. The Gifts are wisdom, understanding, counsel, knowledge, fortitude, piety, and fear of the Lord.

What are the Theological Virtues?

The Theological Virtues of faith, hope, and charity are graces received by God. They have their source in God, are infused in us by him, and as we grow in using them, we are drawn more deeply into the mystery of God.

What are the Cardinal Virtues?

The Cardinal Virtues are qualities acquired by human effort. They are prudence, justice, fortitude, and temperance. All of your moral strengths depend on these virtues. They are rooted in the Theological Virtues given to you by God to help you act as his child.

MY CONFIRMATION JOURNAL

Use your journal to enter more deeply into this chapter. Quietly spend time reflecting and recording on journal pages 41–50.

Words to Know

Cardinal Virtues	justice
charity	knowledge
counsel	piety
faith	prudence
fear of the Lord	temperance
fortitude	Theological Virtues
Gifts of the Holy Spirit	understanding
	wisdom
hope	

REACH OUT

Review the Theological Virtues. Then using pictures from magazines or your own drawings, design a collage that depicts each of the three virtues. When you have finished, write your own act of faith, hope, and love.

WITH MY SPONSOR

Arrange with your sponsor to share your insights, questions, and ideas from this chapter and how they relate to your conversations from the *Faith to Faith* magazine.

Father, Son, and Holy Spirit, be with me, protect me, and guide me. Help me know your will and have the strength and courage to do your will. Amen.

review

GIFTS AND VIRTUES GALLERY

Match each gift or virtue with the phrase that describes a person displaying it.

a. fortitude	**h.** hope
b. faith	**i.** prudence
c. charity	**j.** piety
d. counsel	**k.** temperance
e. justice	**l.** knowledge
f. fear of the Lord	**m.** fortitude
g. wisdom	**n.** understanding

_____ **1.** considers others' needs and values fairness

_____ **2.** recognizes and makes right choices in relationships with God and others

_____ **3.** recognizes God's greatness and our dependence on him

_____ **4.** resists temptation and does what's right even when it's difficult

_____ **5.** knows the meaning of Jesus' teachings

_____ **6.** stops and thinks before acting

_____ **7.** aware of the presence of God in others

_____ **8.** trusts God completely and believes all he has revealed through the Church

_____ **9.** stands up for beliefs and lives as a follower of God

_____ **10.** loves God and neighbor because of God's love for us

_____ **11.** seeks good advice and receives it from others

_____ **12.** sees life from God's point of view

_____ **13.** exhibits self-control and limits desire for enjoyment

_____ **14.** has confidence that God will be with us forever

GIFTS FROM GOD

In the boxes below, write the correct Gift of the Spirit for each definition.

enables you to love God's creation and to see things from his point of view

[ ]

helps you know the value of your life experiences

[ ]

enables you to love and respect God and others

[ ]

gives you strength to stand up for your beliefs

[ ]

gives you insights into the truths of the faith

[ ]

allows you to recognize God's greatness

[ ]

helps you seek advice and be open to the advice of others

[ ]

CHAPTER 6

Confirmed in the
Church

What makes a celebration special for you? Is it the people, the music, the food? What can you do to help everyone feel included?

"[G]rant that we, who are nourished by the Body and Blood of your Son and filled with his Holy Spirit, may become one body, one spirit in Christ." —*Eucharistic Prayer III*

Put On Love

Put on then, as God's chosen ones, holy and beloved, heartfelt compassion, kindness, humility, gentleness, and patience, bearing with one another and forgiving one another, if one has a grievance against another; as the Lord has forgiven you, so must you also do. And over all these put on love, that is, the bond of perfection. And let the peace of Christ control your hearts, the peace into which you were also called in one body. And be thankful. Let the word of Christ dwell in you richly, as in all wisdom you teach and admonish one another, singing psalms, hymns, and spiritual songs with gratitude in your hearts to God. And whatever you do, in word or in deed, do everything in the name of the Lord Jesus, giving thanks to God the Father through him.

Colossians 3:12–17

Understanding Scripture

God the Father cares deeply about our well-being. So he sent his Son, Jesus, to save us. The Letter to the Colossians describes many of the good things God the Father has done for us through Jesus.

In this chapter the virtuous life is described once again as reaching its perfection in love. You are putting on the virtuous life. Now let the peace of Christ fill you as you give thanks to God the Father through Jesus. In him we have become members of a community so united that it is "one body." In this community we are to live in peace and thanksgiving as we do everything in the name of the Lord Jesus.

Scripture and You

Each morning as you put on your clothes, do you ever think about also putting on kindness or gentleness or patience? That's not as easy as it sounds, but fortunately,

you don't have to do it alone. Luckily it is not up to you alone. God the Father and his Son, Jesus, sent the Holy Spirit to help you live in kindness. The peace of Christ and the word of Christ, which dwell in you, also support you in living peacefully.

In the Church we have the seven sacraments, beginning with Baptism, which help us wear love like our favorite clothes. In the Sacrament of Reconciliation, our sins are forgiven; we find pardon and peace. In the Eucharist we share in the very life of Jesus. These two sacraments help us accept and forgive one another as we live lives of peace and thanksgiving.

REFLECTING ON GOD'S WORD

Take some time to center yourself, quietly breathing in and out. Silently reflect on the words *compassion, kindness, humility, gentleness,* and *patience.* Think about which of these qualities you would like God to help you strengthen. Ask for his help now.

Many, Yet One

A young woman serving as a missionary in New Guinea brings Holy Communion to a dying mother. Mexican children sing and clap as they process to church for the feast-day Mass of the patroness of their town, the Virgin of San Juan de los Lagos. Pope Benedict XVI canonizes an Indian nun at a majestic solemn Mass in Rome.

What makes all these people one? How are we united with the Church in New Guinea, Mexico, and Italy? The Church in this world is the sacrament of salvation for all. The Church is the instrument that makes the communion between God and people possible. When we come together to celebrate the Eucharist, we are united with the Church throughout the world and with all the angels and saints as well. We are one through Jesus, the Bread of Life. In the Eucharist our bonds with the worldwide Church are strengthened. We belong not only to our parish community but also to the universal Church.

When we are with our friends, we feel we belong. Every moment is important. We listen intently to what they have to say. We are excited to participate in the conversations. Time goes by quickly, and we make plans to get together again.

Because of our Baptism, we belong to the Body of Christ, the Church, and all the members are our friends in Christ. When we participate in the Eucharist, we strengthen our friendships with Jesus, whose love for us is so great. We worship God, offer together the sacrifice of

ART LINK

Festival of Lights, **John August Swanson, 2000.**

Calvary, and enter into the **Paschal Mystery** of Jesus' life, Death, and Resurrection. Our life as Catholics comes from the Eucharist and leads to the Eucharist. Through the work of the Spirit, the Eucharist helps us love and serve as Jesus did.

Jesus Alive!

The Holy Spirit makes Jesus available to the world. When Mary said yes to God, Jesus was conceived through the power of the Holy Spirit. When the Spirit descended on the disciples at Pentecost, they proclaimed that Jesus was alive in the world. When the Spirit came to you in Baptism, Christ became alive in you. At Mass the Holy Spirit speaks through the Scriptures. Then, in the Eucharistic prayer, the priest prays that through the power of the Holy Spirit, Jesus Christ becomes truly present under the appearance of bread and wine. And Jesus is with us.

The Holy Spirit is the Spirit of Jesus bringing you closer to himself. He makes you one with Jesus in the Mass, when you offer to the Father your joys, sorrows, successes, and failures. The Spirit works in the community that is gathered to receive the Eucharist and unites all members of this community in faith and love.

Liturgy of the Word

The Mass has two main parts: the **Liturgy of the Word** and the **Liturgy of the Eucharist**. Both God's Word and Jesus Christ's Body and Blood unite us and nourish us as People of God.

In the Liturgy of the Word, you are united with other members of God's family. Just as you hear family members' stories when you celebrate with loved ones, you also hear God's stories in the Liturgy of the Word when you gather at Mass.

MY TURN   The Power of God's Word

Reflect on the following readings often used in the Confirmation liturgy. Then write how they speak of unity in believing, living, and proclaiming God's message.

1. *Acts of the Apostles 1:8* "[Y]ou will receive power when the holy Spirit comes upon you, and you will be my witnesses . . ." Name two ways that members of your parish are united as witnesses to Jesus.

_____

_____

2. *Luke 4:18* "The Spirit of the Lord is upon me, because he has anointed me to bring glad tidings to the poor." How can you bring good news to those who are sick, lonely, or in need in other ways?

_____

_____

3. *Luke 10:23* "Blessed are the eyes that see what you see." What can you do to show those who are blind to the needs of others how to love as Jesus loves?

_____

_____

Liturgy of the Eucharist

In the Liturgy of the Eucharist, you are united with Jesus and his sacrifice. You receive the Body and Blood of Christ under the appearance of bread and wine. When you share in the Eucharist, Christ unites you to himself and others. You are one with all who belong to the Church on earth, in Heaven, and in Purgatory. The Eucharist nourishes you to live out the Word of God you have heard proclaimed.

In every liturgy of the Church, God the Father is blessed and adored as the source of all blessings we have received through his Son in order to make us his children through the Holy Spirit.

All That We Have

If you really care about something at school—such as chorus, drama, a club, or a sports team—you get involved. In the same way, caring members of God's family get involved in activities that promote the love of God and others. As fully initiated Christians, we belong to the People of God, which makes it part of our mission to care for people. We are all valuable members of the Body of Christ.

During the Eucharist, we unite our sacrifices to the sacrifice of Jesus. We offer our struggles, successes, and services to the Father. At Mass

we pray for the needs of the Church and the world, and for the coming of the kingdom.

Through service and prayer for the needs of others, we participate in the best way possible. Since the moments spent celebrating the Eucharist are so important, we respond with the community by praying and singing reverently and by receiving Holy Communion.

MY TURN | The Order of Mass

Using pages 104–105 of this book, number the parts of the Mass. Then write *LW* if it is from Liturgy of the Word or *LE* if it is from Liturgy of the Eucharist.

_____ Homily   _____

_____ Eucharistic Prayer   _____

_____ Prayer over   _____
the Offerings

_____ Gospel Reading   _____

_____ Second Reading   _____

_____ Presentation and   _____
Preparation of the Gifts

_____ Prayer of the Faithful   _____

When Things Go Wrong

As you prepare to become a confirmed Catholic, think about the role you play in the community of faith. You are part of a grace-filled Church that is united around the Eucharist and worships God the Father. Because our Church is human, it is capable of sin. Sin is something we do or fail to do that is contradictory to God's law. It is an offense against God and harms our relationship with him and others. Mortal sin, which breaks our relationship with God and others, must be confessed in the Sacrament of Reconciliation. We commit a **mortal sin** when

- we do something that is seriously wrong.

- we freely and willingly choose to do it.

A **venial sin** is a less serious offense that weakens our relationship with God and others. When we are repentant, we are forgiven by prayer, good actions, and receiving Holy Communion. It is recommended that we confess venial sins in the Sacrament of Reconciliation.

Just as the goodness of all in the community strengthens the Body of Christ, so does each of our sins hurts and weakens it. Sin brings division and causes us to be at odds with ourselves, others, and God. When we are wounded by sin, Christ heals us through the Sacrament of Reconciliation.

Like a peacemaker who steps in to break up an argument, Jesus Christ came to bring people together, heal the brokenhearted, lead us to a good relationship with God, and restore what was lost by sin. Christ asks us to forgive one another as he forgives us, and he encourages us to seek forgiveness from him and others. The strength to be healers is given to us by Christ through the Holy Spirit.

rite

Rite

The Sacrament of Confirmation usually takes place in the context of the Eucharist. The Liturgy of the Eucharist is celebrated once the confirmands have been confirmed. All are called to receive the Body and Blood of Jesus Christ in Holy Communion.

Meaning

In receiving the Eucharist, you participate in Christ's self-giving and are united as the Church, the People of God.

Daily Life

When we glorify God through our words and actions, we are sharing his love with others.

Life of Faith

The gifts of faith that we receive in Confirmation are strengthened through celebrating the Eucharist and receiving Holy Communion.

A Forgiving Heart

For seven happy years, Jane de Chantal managed the castle of her husband, Baron Christophe de Rabutin-Chantal. Each day she gathered her family for Mass, and she supervised the household and her children's education. Jane fed people who were poor and showed her children how to love others.

Sadly, Jane's secure home was torn apart by tragedy. Christophe was killed by another man in a hunting accident. Jane tried to be positive and forgiving, but it was very difficult.

One day, Jane met Bishop Francis de Sales. She celebrated the Sacrament of Reconciliation with him and told him about her life. Francis told her that she must trust God more and forgive the man who had accidentally killed her husband. Jane's deep faith helped her forgive the one who had hurt her most. Eventually

Saint Jane de Chantal.

she became a godparent for the man's child. She felt the peace of Christ that comes from a forgiving heart. Later, along with Francis de Sales, Jane founded the Sisters of the Visitation. After three miracles were attributed to her, the Church declared her a saint.

MY TURN — How Can We Be Healers?

Read these stories. Determine who is a healer and who is not.

1. José overheard Matt being corrected by his teacher for trying to steal from another student's desk. When José got to the cafeteria, his classmates wanted to know where Matt was. José said that Matt was busy and changed the subject.

Is José a healer? Why or why not?

_____

_____

2. Beth made fun of Anna in front of her friends by mocking the way she sang at practice. Later, Beth came and apologized. Anna told her coldly, "Sorry isn't enough," and walked away.

Is Beth a healer? Why or why not?

_____

Is Anna a healer? Why or why not?

_____

The Sacrament of Reconciliation

Like Saint Jane de Chantal, we may find it difficult to forgive those who have hurt us. But Jesus calls us to forgive others as we prepare to receive forgiveness of our sins from him. In the Sacrament of Reconciliation, we encounter Jesus and ask him to forgive our sins through the ministry of the priest. We trust in God's mercy and in the forgiveness of others who belong to the community of faith.

The priest represents Jesus and the forgiving community. When we hear his words of **absolution,** our sins are forgiven, and the Church grows stronger and closer together. The divisions caused by our selfishness are healed, and the bonds of the community are strengthened. The priest is bound by the seal of confession never to reveal what anyone confesses.

Dedicated to Liturgy: Blessed Carlos Rodriguez

Carlos Rodriguez was born in Puerto Rico in 1918. When he was in high school, he began to develop health problems that would last his whole life. He left college because of his illness, but he never stopped reading and learning. His great love was to help people understand and love the Mass and the sacraments. Long before the reforms of the Second Vatican Council, Carlos promoted liturgical renewal, which included celebrating the Mass in Spanish so that people could better understand it and therefore participate more fully. Many people began to experience a renewed faith because of Carlos's teaching and the integrity with which he served the Church and others. Carlos Rodriguez died in 1963. In 1999 Pope John Paul II declared him blessed because of the example of his life and his dedication to the liturgy. His feast day is July 13.

Dignity of Work and Rights of Workers

Blessed Carlos Rodriguez dedicated his life's work to make this a better world, according to God's will. We too, through our daily work, participate in the activity of God our Creator. The wonders produced through human work are signs of God's greatness. Since work contributes to a better human society, it is of vital concern to the Kingdom of God. Work gives people a sense of dignity and accomplishment. Work makes it possible for people to be independent and self-reliant. The Church is concerned that all people have the opportunity to work, are paid enough for their work to live decently, have safe and healthy working environments, and are given enough time to rest from work. These are issues that touch all our lives and have a direct connection to our spiritual well-being.

Act of Contrition

Helping people understand the Liturgy of the Church was at the heart of Blessed Carlos's work and mission. A central rite in the Liturgy of the Church is the Sacrament of Reconciliation. Think about a time when you wronged someone. Did you ask for forgiveness? How did you feel after you were forgiven? Now think about a time someone wronged you. Did you forgive the person, even though it was difficult? The Act of Contrition is a prayer we can pray when we are truly sorry for our sins. Through the Act of Contrition, we express our sorrow and ask for God's help. At the beginning of each Mass, we also express our sorrow for the sins we have committed. We do so during the Penitential Act.

Call to Prayer

Ask God for help to avoid sin, and for the strength to forgive those who have wronged us.

Act of Contrition

All: In the name of the Father, and of the Son, and of the Holy Spirit. Amen.

Leader: Gathered as a community of believers, let us listen to God, speaking to us in his Word today and always.

Put on then, as God's chosen ones, holy and beloved, heartfelt compassion, kindness, humility, gentleness, and patience, bearing with one another and forgiving one another, if one has a grievance against another; as the Lord has forgiven you, so must you also do. And over all these put on love, that is, the bond of perfection. And let the peace of Christ control your hearts, the peace into which you were also called in one body. And be thankful. Let the word of Christ dwell in you richly, as in all wisdom you teach and admonish one another, singing psalms, hymns, and spiritual songs with gratitude in your hearts to God. And whatever you do, in word or in deed, do everything in the name of the Lord Jesus, giving thanks to God the Father through him.

Colossians 3:12–17

Leader: Asking for forgiveness is sometimes difficult. But strength in character comes from knowing when we have sinned, being heartfelt in asking for forgiveness, and avoiding whatever leads us to sin. God asks us to be genuine, and we will always be forgiven. The warm embrace of forgiveness brings us peace in our hearts. Now let us pray together the Act of Contrition.

All: My God,
I am sorry for my sins with all my heart.
In choosing to do wrong
and failing to do good,
I have sinned against you
whom I should love above all things.
I firmly intend, with your help,
to do penance,
to sin no more,
and to avoid whatever leads me to sin.
Our Savior Jesus Christ
suffered and died for us.
In his name, my God, have mercy.

Leader: Think about times when you found it difficult to forgive someone or to ask for forgiveness of someone you have wronged. Confirmation helps us build our character so that we can be more like Jesus. Take a few moments now for personal reflection. Speak to God in the quiet of your heart.

All: Loving God, through your gifts, we have the tools we need to be loyal, faithful followers. Please help us find the strength we need when we falter and the grace to recognize when we have done wrong. With your grace, we can be more faithful disciples of Jesus, your Son.
Amen.

summary

FAITH SUMMARY

The Eucharist and the Sacrament of Reconciliation increase the love and unity of the Church. When we participate in the Eucharist, we strengthen our friendships with Jesus, whose love for us is so great. When we are wounded by sin, Christ heals us through the Sacrament of Reconciliation.

REMEMBER

How do the Sacraments of Eucharist and Reconciliation unite the Christian community?

In the Eucharist we celebrate the mystery of Jesus' sacrifice of love and the holy meal that unites us in the Body of Christ. Through the Sacrament of Reconciliation, our sins are forgiven, and we are reconciled with God, the community, and ourselves.

What are the two main parts of the Mass?

The Liturgy of the Word and the Liturgy of the Eucharist are the main parts of the Mass. God's Word and Christ's Body and Blood unite and nourish us as People of God.

Why do we offer ourselves in the Eucharist?

We participate fully in the Eucharist when we offer ourselves and pray for the needs of others. We show how much we trust the power and goodness that comes to us. We do this when we respond, pray, sing, and receive Holy Communion.

How does sin weaken the Body of Christ?

Just as the goodness of all in the community strengthens the Church, so does each of our offenses hurt and weaken it. Sin brings division and causes us to be at odds with ourselves, others, and God. Christ forgives our sins through the Sacrament of Reconciliation.

Words to Know

absolution	mortal sin
Liturgy of the Eucharist	Paschal Mystery
Liturgy of the Word	venial sin

MY CONFIRMATION JOURNAL

Use your journal to enter more deeply into this chapter. Quietly spend time reflecting and recording on journal pages 51–60.

REACH OUT

An examination of conscience is a prayerful review of how we have been living our lives in light of what the Gospel asks of us. It is often based on a reflection on each commandment and on how we have or have not been faithful to that commandment since our last examination. Write an examination of conscience based on 1 Corinthians 13:4–12. You can also use the Examination of Conscience on page 103 of this book.

WITH MY SPONSOR

Arrange with your sponsor to share your insights, questions, and ideas from this chapter and how they relate to your conversations from the *Faith to Faith* magazine.

Loving God, grant me the serenity to accept the things I cannot change; the courage to change the things I can; and wisdom to know the difference. Amen.

review

Fill in the blank lines. When finished, the boxed letters will spell the sacrament that is being described. Write the name of the sacrament on the last blank line.

1. It helps us __ ▓ __ __ love like our

favorite clothes.

2. In it we share in the very life of __ __ __ ▓ __.

3. It helps us live lives of __ __ __ ▓ __.

4. In this sacrament, Jesus becomes

present through the power of the

▓ __ __ __ __ __ __ __ __.

5. Jesus' Body and Blood take the appearance

of __ __ __ ▓ __ and wine.

6. The __ __ __ ▓ __ __ works in the

community gathered for this sacrament.

7. It __ __ __ __ ▓ __ __ __ us as

People of God.

8. The Word of God proclaimed in this

sacrament is the ▓ __ __ __ all over

the world.

9. When we share in it, God unites us to

himself and __ ▓ __ __ __ __.

_____

Place a check mark by the true statements.

_____ **1.** Mortal sin breaks our relationship
with God and others.

_____ **2.** Venial sin weakens our
relationship with God and others.

_____ **3.** Members of Jesus' community
are "one body."

_____ **4.** The Holy Spirit does not make Jesus
present in the world.

_____ **5.** The Spirit makes you one with Jesus.

_____ **6.** The Liturgy of the Word and the
Liturgy of the Eucharist are the two
main parts of the Mass.

_____ **7.** You pray only for your own needs
at Mass.

_____ **8.** It is not important to pray, sing, or
respond during Mass.

_____ **9.** A confirmed Christian is part of a
community that is without grace.

_____ **10.** Our sins are forgiven when we
receive absolution.

*For each definition write the letter of the word
that matches it best.*

a. mortal sin   **d.** Paschal Mystery

b. absolution   **e.** venial sin

c. Liturgy of   **f.** Liturgy of
the Word   the Eucharist

_____ **1.** Jesus' life, Death, Resurrection,
and Ascension

_____ **2.** unites us in one faith to believe in
one God

_____ **3.** unites us with Jesus and his sacrifice

_____ **4.** must be confessed in the Sacrament
of Reconciliation

_____ **5.** the forgiveness of sins

_____ **6.** lesser sins

CHAPTER 7

Confirmed in witness

How do your friends know what is most important to you? If you asked them to name three things that really express who you are, what would they say?

"O God, who have taught the hearts of the faithful by the light of the Holy Spirit, grant that in the same Spirit we may be truly wise . . . " —*Votive Mass of the Holy Spirit*

One Spirit, Many Forms of Service

There are different kinds of spiritual gifts but the same Spirit; there are different forms of service but the same Lord; there are different workings but the same God who produces all of them in everyone. To each individual the manifestation of the Spirit is given for some benefit. To one is given through the Spirit the expression of wisdom; to another the expression of knowledge according to the same Spirit; to another faith by the same Spirit; to another gifts of healing by the one Spirit; to another mighty deeds; to another prophecy; to another discernment of spirits; to another varieties of tongues; to another interpretation of tongues. But one and the same Spirit produces all of these, distributing them individually to each person as he wishes.

As a body is one though it has many parts, and all the parts of the body, though many, are one body, so also Christ. For in one Spirit we were all baptized into one body, whether Jews or Greeks, slaves or free persons, and we were all given to drink of one Spirit.

1 Corinthians 12:4–13

Understanding Scripture

The passage above deals with the Church in Corinth. It was made up of a variety of people: Romans, Greeks, and Jews; rich people and poor people; citizens and noncitizens; free people and slaves. After Paul began this church, he left to begin churches in other cities. When he heard from his friends in Corinth that things were not going well, he wrote them letters such as this one. Paul is reminding the people that they are different from one another. But all are baptized into the one Body of Christ. They all have different gifts to share. All their spiritual gifts were given to them by the Holy Spirit and were meant to build the community, not to divide it. Whatever their gifts, they are meant to be used for the good of all.

Scripture and You

In your preparation for Confirmation, you have been growing in your understanding of your faith, considering ways you can live as a better follower of Jesus', and thinking about how to use the gifts you have been given. Ask yourself, What form of service can I give to others? Each of us has been given different gifts. How can you best share your gifts with others?

REFLECTING ON GOD'S WORD

Relax and close your eyes. Reflect on your friends. Think about the different gifts they have to offer. Thank God for all this variety. Ask him to help you use your gifts to the best of your ability.

Ready to Witness

After your Confirmation you may not be automatically wiser. You probably won't be speaking in tongues or healing people. You will probably feel about the same as you did before Confirmation. Your growth in the Spirit will be a lifelong journey. But the same Holy Spirit who came to the early Christians on Pentecost also strengthens you for your mission.

The time after your Confirmation is especially important. You can fulfill your prophetic mission to be a witness to Christ in all circumstances and at the very heart of the human community. You can participate in the Eucharist, and in the Sacrament of Reconciliation, pray, perform works of mercy, and live a courageous and faithful Christian life in your community and beyond. During this time the community of faith will continue to support you and encourage you to share your gifts and talents in loving service for Christ.

A Plan for Spiritual Growth

Here are some suggestions for living as disciples of Christ and continuing your spiritual growth. Think about how you will apply them to your life and make a firm commitment to do so.

Eucharist

Participating in the Eucharist is the most important part of your week.

- Prepare to offer your struggles and successes with Christ, and receive him in the Eucharist.

- Pray at the Eucharistic liturgy for a greater love for Christ and others.

- After Mass reflect on the readings or the Homily.

- Throughout the week, live out your commitment to your faith.

ART LINK

Gaston de La Touche, *The Last Supper* (detail), 1897.

Reconciliation

Receiving God's loving forgiveness on a regular basis.

- Reflect daily on your words and actions toward God, others, and yourself.

- Take time to do an examination of conscience.

- Participate in the Sacrament of Reconciliation in your parish.

- Strive continually to grow closer to God.

Prayer

Your relationship with God is nurtured through communication.

- Read about God's love for you in the Scriptures.

- Take time during your day to talk to God in prayer.

- Write your reflections in your journal.

- Pray the Rosary.

Works of Charity

Jesus showed us what a life of loving service means.

- Practice the Corporal and Spiritual Works of Mercy.

- Show concern for those who are poor and in need.

- Be of service at home, in school, and in your parish.

- Be a good steward of your gifts, time, and resources.

Community

You share a common vision and love for Christ and for other members of his body, the Church.

- Recognize when you need to be reconciled with anyone.

- Participate actively, fully, and consciously in your parish liturgies.

- Share your faith and grow in it by participating in the parish youth group, Bible study, or any other parish activity.

MY TURN   What Can You Contribute?

Make a list of at least three acts or works of charity that you can perform.

_____

_____

_____

_____

_____

_____

_____

_____

Fruits of the Spirit

When you live united to Christ and follow the guidance of the Holy Spirit, your life bears the fruit of good works. You will be aware of God dwelling in you by the joy you experience in doing good. People will recognize God's presence in you by seeing your good works, your love for others, and your service to them.

Based on his letter to the Galatians, Saint Paul wrote, "[T]he fruit of the Spirit is love, joy, peace, patience, kindness, generosity, faithfulness, gentleness, self-control." (Galatians 5:22–23) To this list, Church Tradition has added goodness, modesty, and chastity. These are the 12 **Fruits of the Spirit**. They are the result of the Spirit's presence in a believing person. They are also the result of cooperating with God's grace.

Read the following descriptions of the 12 Fruits of the Spirit and the stories that follow. Find evidence of the Fruits of the Spirit in the stories. Think about how people might find evidence of some of them in your life.

Faithfulness

Keep your promises. You show **faithfulness** when you show loyalty to God and to those to whom you have committed yourself. Faithful people are dependable, trustworthy, and obedient.

Goodness

Goodness flows from God's great love. It is a sign that you love all people without exception and do good to them.

Love

Love, or charity, is shown in selfless service to others by your words and actions. Love is a sign that you love God and that you love others as Jesus loves you.

A Man Who Loved God and Others

If you went into the Berard family's hairdressing shop in Manhattan in the early 1800s, you received much more than a shave and a haircut. Pierre Toussaint, an enslaved man who was Catholic, worked for the family and was skilled at his trade. Day after day he listened to people's heartaches and family stories as he cut their hair. Time after time he would speak to his customers about Jesus, Mary, and the importance of loving others. Pierre was never too tired after work to care for those who were poor. He used much of the money he made to buy the freedom of other enslaved people rather than spending it to buy his own freedom. Pierre was an ordinary person who showed other ordinary people how to be holy. He was faithful to his baptismal promises. Pierre was a man who showed by his actions that he loved God and others. Pope John Paul II declared him venerable in 1996.

Venerable Pierre Toussaint.

Modesty

Modesty is moderation in all your actions, especially your conversation and external behavior. Modesty is a sign that you give credit to God for your talents and successes.

Modesty is an attitude that protects what is most personal to us, refusing to reveal that which should remain private. It guides the way a person looks at others and acts toward them, respecting the dignity of others.

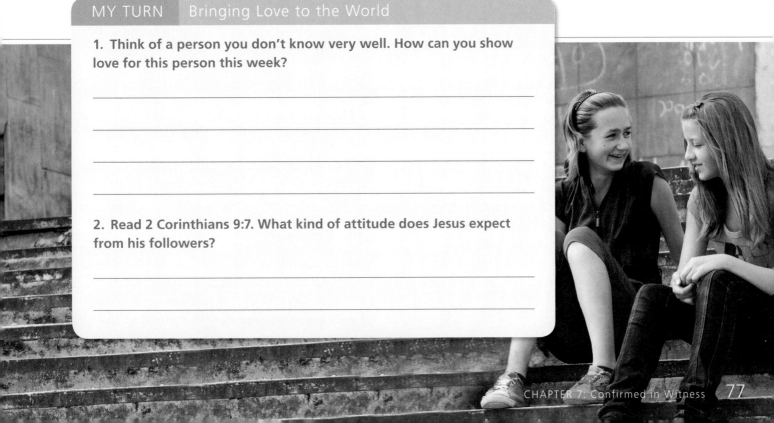

| MY TURN | Bringing Love to the World |

1. Think of a person you don't know very well. How can you show love for this person this week?

_____

_____

_____

_____

2. Read 2 Corinthians 9:7. What kind of attitude does Jesus expect from his followers?

_____

_____

Kindness

Kindness is shown by generous acts of service. Kind people are compassionate and considerate. They see the best in others.

A Nurse from God

An old woman climbed the last step of the staircase and leaned against the wall, gasping for breath. She knocked on the door, which was opened by a refined, red-haired woman in a gray dress. "Excuse me, ma'am. They said you were a nurse and could help me," said the old lady. "If you can't, they'll send me to die on Blackwell Island." (Blackwell Island in New York housed a state-run asylum.)

The old woman said she would pay her when she was able. "Nonsense," said the red-haired woman, whose name was Rose Hawthorne. "If you had the money, you could go to the hospital. I help those who can't pay." Rose gently unwrapped the bandage to reveal a cancerous wound on the woman's face. Rose's hands worked quickly to clean the sore.

The old woman commented that Rose was very kind and that she must come from a nice family. "I do come from a nice family," Rose replied, "God's family. You're part of that family too. And in God's family, we help one another."

Rose Hawthorne helped the poorest and most unloved of God's family. In the early 1900s, she began caring for neglected people in New York who were forced to die on Blackwell Island. Eventually she founded an order of Dominican sisters who cared for patients with incurable cancer.

Rite

At the conclusion of the rite, we are dismissed and sent forth to spread the Word of God.

Meaning

The presence of the Holy Spirit is symbolized by wind. Just as the wind blows everywhere, we are called to spread the Good News everywhere. We are to carry Christ's message throughout the world by our words and actions, and by using our gifts in service to others. We are God's messengers of faith and love.

Daily Life

As we carry and spread God's love through the world, the Spirit works through us and in us.

Life of Faith

At Mass we ask the Holy Spirit to be with us and guide us—now, and in the days ahead.

Self-Control

You can discipline your physical and emotional desires by being modest and respectful of others. With **self-control** you can be in charge of your emotions and desires instead of the other way around.

Patience

We are confronted with difficulties on a daily basis. **Patience** is love that is willing to endure life's suffering and difficulties, the routine and the unexpected. It means not giving up in difficult or unwelcome situations.

A Mother's Patience

Angelo Roncalli was not the best or most hard-working student as a young man. His mother often had to remind him to finish his schoolwork. But she never gave up on him.

Decades later, Angelo, as Pope John XXIII, would have made his mother very proud. He persevered in school, and he was well-educated and understood God's people. He called the Second Vatican Council to renew the Church and help it address the concerns of the 20th century. Many of his advisors protested the idea of Church renewal. They were not convinced that renewal was needed. Pope John XXIII accepted their opposition with patience, but he did not give up. He knew that God would guide the Council. Even when Pope John XXIII faced an unfinished Council before he died, he could smile peacefully and say calmly, "God will take care." John XXIII was beatified in the year 2000.

Blessed John XXIII.

Peace

Jesus said to his disciples on Easter morning, "Peace I give you." A disciple faithful to God's will is serene, not overly anxious or upset. **Peace** comes from knowing that all will work out well because God is with us.

Joy

Joy is a deep and constant gladness in the Lord that circumstances cannot destroy. It comes from a good relationship with God and others—a relationship of genuine love.

MY TURN   A Need for Peace

1. Which type of peace (world, family, personal) do you see as the greatest need? Write a petition expressing your hopes for peace.

_____

_____

2. Imagine you are writing a book, called *How to Be Patient*, to help young people grow spiritually. Suggest four ways to practice patience.

_____

_____

_____

_____

Paper cranes, a symbol of world peace.

Chastity

Chastity is being faithful to one's sexuality in conduct and intention. It helps us live out our sexuality in a proper manner. For example, married people are celibate to the entire world except for one person—their spouse. All people, married and single, are called to practice chastity.

A Chaste Couple
Luigi and Maria Beltrame Quattrocchi were a married couple who raised four children and led active lives of Christian service. On October 21, 2001, at the Mass declaring them blesseds, Pope John Paul II said, "The richness of faith and married love shown by Luigi and Maria is a living demonstration of what the Second Vatican Council said about all the faithful being called to holiness."

Through their love for each other, Luigi and Maria gave to others. Together they were a family that was open to prayer, friendship, and solidarity with those who were poor. Their shared feast day is November 25, their wedding anniversary.

Gentleness

Strength tempered by love leads you to be gentle, peaceful, and gracious. A person showing **gentleness** has the power to forgive instead of getting angry.

Generosity

Generosity is a willingness to give even at a cost to yourself. It expresses concern for meeting the needs of others even if it means sacrificing something of your own.

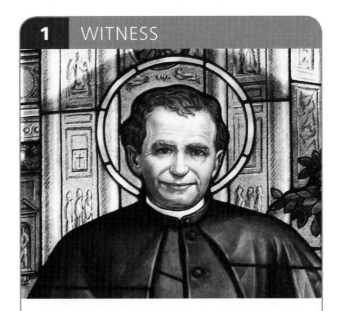

1 WITNESS

Advocate for Young People: Saint John Bosco

John Bosco was born in Italy in 1815. At that time, many boys were orphaned and poor. Without families and religious training, these boys often got into fights, stole, and hurt others. As a young boy, Bosco taught the Good News of Jesus' love to other boys and persuaded them to go to Mass. Later, he decided to join the priesthood. Priests at the seminary saw that Bosco was a natural leader, and that he was filled with the Holy Spirit. The priests encouraged Bosco to use his gifts to help other young people. He began gathering boys together on Sundays for Mass and catechism lessons. The day would also include food, games, and evening prayers. Later, Bosco started a home for orphaned or neglected boys. He opened workshops to train boys to be skilled in a trade, and he also wrote and published books on Christian faith for boys. In 1859, Bosco instituted a religious community of priests who took care of neglected boys. The Salesians, named after Francis de Sales, are still active today. Saint John Bosco is an excellent example of the Gifts of the Holy Spirit in action. His feast day is January 31.

Solidarity

Saint John Bosco witnessed boys in great physical, emotional, and spiritual need, and he wanted to help them. He taught them about Jesus and gave them a second chance to lead good, productive lives. Need is not something that exists only on the other side of the world. There is need right outside our door. We can make a difference and help improve the lives of people in our local community. As we grow in faith in God, who is Truth and Love, we grow in solidarity with people all over the world. Faith does not isolate us or divide us. It makes us more aware of the interdependence among individuals and among nations. In Jesus we see the immeasurable love of God. He takes on our difficulties, walks with us, saves us, and makes us one in him. In him, life in society, with all its difficulties, becomes an invitation to be more involved in sharing. In the light of faith, solidarity is linked to forgiveness and reconciliation.

witness

The Golden Rule

The Golden Rule says we should treat others as we would want to be treated. It represents the kind of attitude that should be found in someone who is responding to God's love as revealed in Jesus Christ. Jesus tells us that everything we do for others we also do for him. Do you follow the Golden Rule in your daily life? How would the world change if everyone followed the Golden Rule?

Call to Prayer

Ask God to guide you in doing good and always being our best selves, serving others and serving Jesus.

Holy Spirit mosaic, Ukraine.

fruits

Fruits of the Holy Spirit

All: In the name of the Father, and of the Son, and of the Holy Spirit. Amen.

Leader: Gathered as a community of believers, let us listen to God, speaking to us in his Word today and always.

There are different kinds of spiritual gifts but the same Spirit; there are different forms of service but the same Lord; there are different workings but the same God who produces all of them in everyone. To each individual the manifestation of the Spirit is given for some benefit. . . .

As a body is one though it has many parts, and all the parts of the body, though many, are one body, so also Christ. For in one Spirit we were all baptized into one body, whether Jews or Greeks, slaves or free persons, and we were all given to drink of one Spirit.

1 Corinthians 12:4–7,12–13

Leader: Like Saint Paul said, "The Church is one body but with many parts." We are strong as a community of believers, on whom the Spirit has bestowed many gifts. Let us be mindful of the gifts we have received, and ask God that we might use them to serve the Lord and one another.

Reader 1: We are called to be faithful to God and those to whom we have committed ourselves.

Reader 2: To serve others by our words and actions.

Reader 3: To love all, without exception, and to do good.

All: May we bear the fruits of faithfulness, love, and goodness.

Reader 1: We are called to be compassionate and considerate.

Reader 2: To be gracious, gentle, and forgiving.

Reader 3: To be generous and selfless.

All: May we bear the fruits of kindness, gentleness, and generosity.

Reader 1: We are called to be aware of our emotions and desires and to use them wisely.

Reader 2: To honor and respect the gift of our bodies.

Reader 3: To show moderation in our behavior and conversations.

All: May we bear the fruits of self-control, chastity, and modesty.

Reader 1: We are called to endure lovingly the many situations we encounter in life.

Reader 2: To be peacemakers.

Reader 3: To share our joy with others.

All: May we bear the fruits of patience, peace, and joy.

Leader: Loving Father, thank you for all the gifts you have given us. May we be open to them and use them in service to you and all others. Amen.

summary

FAITH SUMMARY

The Fruits of the Spirit are enjoyed by those who wisely use the gifts that we have received from the Holy Spirit.

REMEMBER

How can you nurture your relationship with God?

Your relationship with God can grow through talking and listening to him in prayer. Reading the Bible and recording your thoughts in your journal will help improve your prayer life.

What are the Fruits of the Spirit?

The Fruits of the Spirit are the result of the Spirit's presence, and gifts in a believing person. They are the result of cooperating with God's grace. The Fruits are love, joy, peace, patience, kindness, generosity, faithfulness, gentleness, self-control, goodness, modesty, and chastity.

How can you recognize the Fruits of the Spirit?

You can recognize the Fruits of the Holy Spirit in yourself by the happiness you experience in doing good. Others become aware of the Spirit's presence in you by witnessing your good works.

MY CONFIRMATION JOURNAL

Use your journal to enter more deeply into this chapter. Quietly spend time reflecting and recording on journal pages 61–70.

Words to Know

chastity	joy
faithfulness	kindness
Fruits of the Spirit	love
	modesty
generosity	patience
gentleness	peace
goodness	self-control

REACH OUT

1. Look up other signs of the Spirit found in 1 Timothy 4:12; 1 Timothy 6:11; 2 Timothy 2:22–24; 1 Peter 3:8; and Ephesians 5:8–9. Write how some of these are evident in your parish community.

2. As a fully-initiated Catholic, you will be thinking about your mission, or vocation, in life. Interview a single person, a married couple (perhaps your parents), and a priest or sister about how they experienced their call. Record and transcribe the interview.

3. Write about how Scripture, prayer, the sacraments, or the examples of other Christians can help you practice self-control.

WITH MY SPONSOR

Arrange with your sponsor to share your insights, questions, and ideas from this chapter and how they relate to your conversations from the *Faith to Faith* magazine.

Loving Father, we thank you for all the gifts that you have given us. We ask you to help us use them in loving service to you and all others. Amen.

review

DESCRIBING A CATHOLIC YOUTH

Imagine you are a reporter. On a separate sheet of paper, briefly summarize a day in the life of a Catholic person your age. The person can be real or fictional.

MAKE IT TRUE

*Write **T** for True or **F** for False. Then fix the false statements to make them true.*

_____ **1.** Jesus' example of how to live included practicing acts of mercy and caring for the poor.

_____ **2.** Your relationship with God is nurtured through communication.

_____ **3.** Paul's letter to the Galatians names all the fruits recognized by the Church today.

_____ **4.** Faithfulness is the sign that you love God and that you love others as Jesus did.

_____ **5.** Modesty is moderation in all your actions.

_____ **6.** Kindness is shown by serving others with generosity.

_____ **7.** Modesty shows that you love all people without exception and do good to them.

_____ **8.** Peace comes from not knowing how things will work out.

_____ **9.** Patience is love that is willing to endure suffering.

_____ **10.** You can't discipline your physical desire by being modest and respectful to others.

SEARCHING FOR FRUIT

Circle the hidden Fruits of the Holy Spirit.

goodness	love	joy
modesty	gentleness	self-control
kindness	peace	chastity
faithfulness	generosity	patience

```
L X K C O N G C R Y S X A Y
E O D I J J H K T F S D K T
T F R I N Y C I O P E M E I
G P S T P D S B A I N C S T
P O Q N N O N T U W E R Y S
P M Q E R O I E V P L E E A
Q F L E Z E C I S B T C Q H
M U N B N C Y F E S N A I C
E E Q C X I X T L H E E T T
G O E U G X K N S E G P P Y
Y G O O D N E S S E S U O H
O X L S X C K O N C D J Y H
E V O L A H C E O H E O A A
S S E N L U F H T I A F M Y
```

CHAPTER 8

Confirmed in
grace

What can you do now that you couldn't do when you were seven? How are things different for you now? What do you like best about who you are now?

"Lord, send us your Holy Spirit to help us walk in unity of faith and grow in the strength of his love to the full stature of Christ." –*Rite of Confirmation*

Baptized in the Holy Spirit

While Apollos was in Corinth, Paul traveled through the interior of the country and came [down] to Ephesus where he found some disciples. He said to them, "Did you receive the holy Spirit when you became believers?" They answered him, "We have never even heard that there is a holy Spirit." He said, "How were you baptized?" They replied, "With the baptism of John." Paul then said, "John baptized with a baptism of repentance, telling the people to believe in the one who was to come after him, that is, in Jesus." When they heard this, they were baptized in the name of the Lord Jesus. And when Paul laid [his] hands on them, the holy Spirit came upon them, and they spoke in tongues and prophesied.

Acts of the Apostles 19:1–6

Understanding Scripture

Paul's mission was to preach the Good News of Jesus to the Gentiles. In the Scripture passage above, Paul meets some Jews who had been followers of John the Baptist and then followers of Jesus. But they had only been baptized by John, as Jesus had been. Their baptism of repentance by John needed to be completed by Baptism into the life, Death, Resurrection and Ascension of Jesus. With this Baptism they would receive the Holy Spirit. After they were baptized in the name of the Lord Jesus, Paul laid his hands on them, and they received the Holy Spirit. This gift was expressed in the wondrous acts they were then capable of performing.

Scripture and You

You were probably baptized as an infant and haven't thought much about it since then. Like the believers above, you may have taken your Baptism for granted. But in your preparation for Confirmation, you have been asked to think more seriously about what your Baptism means to you. You received the Holy Spirit at your Baptism, and he will be strengthened in you through the Sacrament of Confirmation.

REFLECTING ON GOD'S WORD

Take a few moments to quiet yourself. Imagine that you are back at the day of your Baptism. Your parents and godparents are there with you as the priest baptizes you. Give thanks to God for your Baptism and for the gift of the Holy Spirit you received at that time. Speak to God silently about whatever you would like.

As You Grow

Your life has changed as you've grown older and matured. You've learned things, developed skills, and become more independent. With this growth comes additional privileges and responsibilities. For example, very little was expected of you as a baby. But you were asked to do a great deal more as a seven-year-old, and even more now.

Spiritual Growth

Just as you grow in strength, size, and intelligence, so are you called to grow in the Holy Spirit. At Baptism you received the gift of grace, or divine life. As you've grown, you've been called to recognize God's love for you and the great gifts he has given you. Now you are ready to accept the responsibilities and privileges that are yours because of your Baptism. Now you have the opportunity to live out your anointing by the Holy Spirit, and to share more fully in the mission of Jesus.

Confirmation

Confirmation celebrates the gift of the Spirit that you received in Baptism. To be confirmed you "should be in the state of grace (that is, without serious sin), be well prepared by catechesis and prayer, and be committed to the responsibilities entailed by the Sacrament." (*United States Catholic Catechism for Adults,* Chapter 16) In Confirmation the Spirit gives you strength to live by God's teachings more fully, to imitate Christ more closely, and to express your faith more courageously. You are bound more closely to the Church in Confirmation so you must be ready to assume the role of disciple and witness to him. The whole community celebrates with you as you commit to Jesus and his Church. The community prays that the Spirit will bless you with the grace

Mary of Pentecost, Cerezo Barredo, 1994.

you need to grow in Christ. Confirmation is celebrated during the Eucharist to express more clearly the unity of the Sacraments of Initiation.

The bishop is the ordinary minister of Confirmation. He receives the fullness of the Sacrament of Holy Orders and shares in the apostolic responsibility and mission of the whole Church.

The Rite of Confirmation

The Rite of Confirmation includes the following parts: the Presentation of the Candidates, Homily, Renewal of Baptismal Promises, Laying On of Hands, Anointing with Chrism, and Prayer of the Faithful.

The Confirmation Mass

Like other liturgical celebrations in which you have participated, the Mass for your Confirmation follows a set pattern. It begins with the **Collect**, or opening prayer.

Presentation of the Candidates

After the Scripture readings, you are presented to the bishop for Confirmation. You are called by name or as a group. By standing before the bishop, you give witness to your desire to declare yourself a Christian and to live as one.

Homily

After the pastor presents you to the bishop, you are seated and the bishop speaks to you and to the congregation in his Homily. In the Homily the bishop explains how the Scripture readings reveal a deeper understanding of the mystery of Confirmation.

Renewal of Baptismal Promises

At the end of the Homily, you publicly renew your baptismal promises by standing and affirming your commitment as a follower of Jesus. You are asked if you reject Satan and all his works. You respond, "I do" to this and to all the basic statements of what we believe as Catholics.

MY TURN   Sending the Spirit

Any of the following can serve as the opening prayer for the Rite of Confirmation. Which of these prayers best summarizes what your Confirmation means to you? Why?

1. God of power and mercy, send your Holy Spirit to live in our hearts and make us temples of his glory.

2. Lord, fulfill your promise: send the Holy Spirit to make us witnesses before the world to the Good News proclaimed by Jesus Christ our Lord.

3. Lord, send us your Holy Spirit to help us walk in unity of faith and grow in the strength of his love to the full stature of Christ.

4. Lord, fulfill the promise given by your Son and send the Holy Spirit to enlighten our minds and lead us to all truth.

_____

_____

_____

_____

After your profession of faith, the bishop invites everyone to pray with him. He says,

My dear friends:
in baptism God our Father gave
*   the new birth of eternal life*
to his chosen sons and daughters.
Let us pray to our Father
that he will pour out the Holy Spirit
to strengthen his sons and daughters
*   with his gifts*
and anoint them to be more like
*   Christ the Son of God.*

Laying On of Hands

As the bishop extends his hands over you in the Rite of Confirmation, your parents, sponsors, and the entire congregation are united in focusing on one thought: Come, Holy Spirit.

The bishop prays,

All-powerful God, Father of
*   our Lord Jesus Christ,*
by water and the Holy Spirit
you freed your sons and daughters from sin
and gave them new life.

Send your Holy Spirit upon them
to be their Helper and Guide.

Give them the spirit of wisdom
*   and understanding,*
the spirit of right judgment and courage,
the spirit of knowledge and reverence.

Fill them with the spirit of
*   wonder and awe in your presence.*

We ask this through Christ our Lord.

MY TURN   The Spirit's Gifts

Which of the Spirit's gifts listed in the prayer will most help you? In what ways?

_____

_____

_____

_____

_____

_____

_____

_____

_____

Anointing with Chrism

In the Rite of Confirmation, you come before the bishop with your sponsor, and your sponsor places his or her hand on your right shoulder. You or your sponsor tells the bishop your Confirmation name.

The bishop confirms you by anointing you with Chrism, done by the laying on of the hand, and with the words, "[Name], be sealed with the Gift of the Holy Spirit."

You respond, "Amen."

Then the bishop extends to you a sign of peace and says, "Peace be with you."

You respond, "And with your spirit."

With the bishop's anointing, you receive an **indelible,** or permanent, character that signifies the way you are sealed with the Gift of the Holy Spirit. The Gift helps you become more like Christ and commissions you to live your prophetic mission to be a witness to him in all circumstances and at the very heart of the human community.

rite

Rite

At Confirmation you receive and celebrate the transforming grace of the Holy Spirit.

Meaning

At Pentecost, the Holy Spirit came to the first Apostles and appeared as tongues of fire above their heads.

Daily Life

The Gift of the Holy Spirit awakens in us new strength and purpose. We can tap into that strength whenever we are faced with a difficult decision or task.

Life of Faith

The Sacrament of Confirmation sets our hearts afire. We pray that we may use the gifts we have received, feel strengthened, give abundant fruits, and be faithful followers of Christ.

Prayer of the Faithful

The Mass continues with intercessions offered for all our needs. In the liturgy you and the other newly confirmed, who have been united in the Gift of the Spirit, are bound together in the worship of the Father through his Son, Jesus Christ.

The Mass Continues

You are joined more closely with one another in praying the Lord's Prayer, in sharing the sign of Christ's peace, and in receiving the Body and Blood of Christ in Holy Communion. When you participate in the Eucharist, you celebrate the life of faith that has been confirmed in you through the action of the Holy Spirit.

The Mass ends with a solemn final blessing prayer over all the people in the assembly. The bishop extends his hands over all and prays the following blessing, or one similar to it.

Bishop: God our Father made you his children by water and the Holy Spirit: may he bless you and watch over you with his fatherly love.

Response: Amen.

Bishop: Jesus Christ the Son of God promised that the Spirit of truth will be with his Church for ever: may he bless you and give you courage in professing the true faith.

Response: Amen.

Bishop: The Holy Spirit came down upon the disciples and set their hearts on fire with love: may he bless you, keep you one in faith and love and bring you to the joy of God's kingdom.

Response: Amen.

Bishop: May almighty God bless you, the Father, and the Son, and the Holy Spirit.

Response: Amen.

MY TURN — Blessed by the Trinity

1. **Review the prayer of solemn final blessing above. Write what each Person of the Trinity did for us or for the disciples.**

_____

_____

_____

2. **Write what each Person of the Trinity will do for us.**

_____

_____

_____

Living Your Commitment

When you are anointed, sealed, and blessed in Confirmation, you assume the role of witness to Jesus in the Church and in the world. By cooperating with the Holy Spirit, you will grow in the knowledge and love of Jesus.

The effects of Confirmation are many.

- You are united closer to Christ.

- The Gifts of the Holy Spirit you received in Baptism are sealed and strengthened.

- You are filled with the Holy Spirit, who will help you accept the new responsibilities you have as a Christian.

- You are better able to participate in the worship and apostolic life of the Church.

What can you add to this list?

Your preparation for the Sacrament of Confirmation is drawing to a close. Take time to thank God and your sponsor for supporting you and guiding you during this special time.

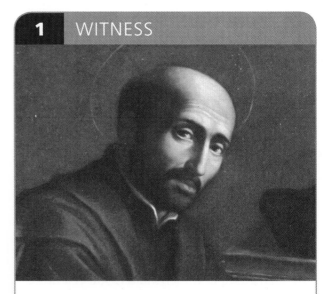

1 WITNESS

Led By the Spirit: Saint Ignatius of Loyola

Ignatius was the youngest son in a noble family in Spain. He joined the military and defended his country for several years. At the age of 30, he was seriously injured in battle. During his recovery, Ignatius asked for some books to read. The only books that could be found were on the life of Christ and the lives of the saints. Reading and thinking about these lives moved Ignatius deeply. He contemplated his own life and experienced a religious conversion. Led by the Spirit, Ignatius decided to give up his military life, return to school, and dedicate his life to God. At the University of Paris, he met six young men who joined him in forming a religious community. They took the three traditional vows of poverty, chastity, and obedience, plus a fourth vow of obedience to the pope. The community's main work was teaching; the priests became great missionaries and were a strong force in fighting false teachings. Today this community is known as the Society of Jesus, or the Jesuits. Ignatius taught that we can find God in all things; God is in everything we see, hear, and do. Saint Ignatius of Loyola's feast day is July 31.

2 ACT

Care for God's Creation

Saint Ignatius taught that God can be found in everyone, in every place, and in everything. When we learn to pay more attention to God, we become more thankful and reverent, and through this we become more devoted to God, more deeply in love with our Creator. Our faith has always urged moderation in the use of material goods. We must not allow our desires for more material things to overtake our concern for the basic needs of people and the environment. A life focused less on material gain may remind us that we are more than what we own. A greater awareness of justice and the common good and a renewed sense of restraint on our part can make an essential contribution to our care for God's creation.

3 PRAY

God's Great Love

God's love is everywhere and in everything. As you complete your preparation for Confirmation, remember that the Holy Spirit is always with you, accompanying you on your faith journey.

Call to Prayer

You will soon receive the Sacrament of Confirmation. Your relationship with God will be stronger. Thank God for his guidance during this important time.

God's Kind and Generous Love

All: In the name of the Father, and of the Son, and of the Holy Spirit. Amen.

Leader: As the day of Confirmation approaches, let us listen to God's Word and pray for one another.

. . . Paul traveled through the interior of the country and came [down] to Ephesus where he found some disciples. He said to them, "Did you receive the holy Spirit when you became believers?" They answered him, "We have never even heard that there is a holy Spirit." He said, "How were you baptized?" They replied, "With the baptism of John." Paul then said, "John baptized with a baptism of repentance, telling the people to believe in the one who was to come after him, that is, in Jesus." When they heard this, they were baptized in the name of the Lord Jesus. And when Paul laid [his] hands on them, the holy Spirit came upon them, and they spoke in tongues and prophesied.

Acts of the Apostles 19:1–6

All: Thanks be to God.

Leader: Let us pray for all those preparing for Confirmation. May they remain faithful to God, give bold witness to the Gospel, and become heirs in the hope of eternal life.

Reader 1: For all of us, sons and daughters of God, that confirmed by the gift of the Spirit we will give witness to Christ by lives built on faith and love. Let us pray to the Lord.

All: Lord, hear our prayer.

Reader 2: For our parents and godparents, who lead us in faith, that by word and example they may always encourage us to follow the way of Jesus. Let us pray to the Lord.

All: Lord, hear our prayer.

Reader 3: For all members of the Church, that God, who gathers us together by the Holy Spirit, may help us grow in unity of faith and love until Jesus, his Son, returns in glory. Let us pray to the Lord.

All: Lord, hear our prayer.

Leader: May the work of the Holy Spirit begun at Pentecost continue to grow in the hearts of all who believe.

All: Amen.

Leader: Today we celebrate the next step in building our relationship with God. Let us think about all we have learned and gained in growing closer to God through preparation for the Sacrament of Confirmation.

All: Loving God, through your gifts we are prepared to serve as people for you and people for others. We are ready, Lord, to live out our responsibilities as confirmed Catholics. Amen.

summary

FAITH SUMMARY

In Confirmation the Spirit empowers us to live God's life more fully and witness to our faith more courageously.

REMEMBER

What is the connection between the Sacraments of Baptism and Confirmation?

The Sacrament of Confirmation perfects baptismal grace, affirms the responsibilities and privileges that you received in Baptism, and celebrates the gift of the Spirit given to you at Baptism.

Why does the Rite of Confirmation take place during a Mass?

When you receive the Eucharist, you participate in and celebrate the faith life that has been confirmed in you through the Holy Spirit. Celebrating Confirmation during the Eucharist expresses the unity of the Sacraments of Initiation.

What are the main parts of the Rite of Confirmation?

The main parts of the Rite of Confirmation are the Presentation of the Candidates, Homily, Renewal of Baptismal Promises, Laying On of Hands, Anointing with Chrism, and the Prayer of the Faithful.

What do you express when you stand before the bishop during the presentation of candidates?

When you stand before the bishop, you give witness to your desire to declare yourself ready to be a disciple and witness of Christ and to live according to his example of love for God and others.

What does the bishop do to confirm you?

The bishop anoints you on the forehead with Chrism and says: "[Name], be sealed with the Gift of the Holy Spirit."

MY CONFIRMATION JOURNAL

Use your journal to enter more deeply into this chapter. Quietly spend time reflecting and recording on journal pages 71–80. Be sure to complete pages 81–83 at the end of your journal.

REACH OUT

1. How do you plan to "live out" your Confirmation? What are your hopes and goals as a Confirmed Catholic? How will you put into practice what you have learned? Write about it.

2. Below are some suggested readings for Confirmation. Which reading speaks the most to you? Why? Write about it.
   - Isaiah 11:1–4
   - Acts of the Apostles 1:3–8
   - Ezekiel 36:24–28
   - Ephesians 4:1–6

WITH MY SPONSOR

Arrange with your sponsor to share your insights, questions, and ideas from this chapter and how they relate to your conversations from the *Faith to Faith* magazine.

Loving God, through the Gifts of the Holy Spirit, we can better serve others. We are ready, Lord, to live out our responsibilities as confirmed Catholics. Amen.

review

Number the steps in the Confirmation Mass in the order they occur.

_____ **1.** Homily

_____ **2.** Readings from Scripture

_____ **3.** Laying On of Hands

_____ **4.** Prayer of the Faithful

_____ **5.** Renewal of Baptismal Promises

_____ **6.** Presentation of the Candidates

_____ **7.** Anointing with Chrism

CONFIRMATION CROSSING

Use the clues to complete this crossword puzzle about the Rite of Confirmation.

Across

6. Three of these—Baptism, Confirmation, and the Eucharist—initiate you as a Christian.

7. The bishop anoints you with this.

8. You become more like Christ when you grow this way.

9. The Spirit keeps them active in you.

Down

1. During the laying on of hands, the bishop _____.

2. You declare yourself this.

3. The Spirit helps you become more like him.

4. Confirmation takes place during this celebration to express the unity of the Sacraments of Initiation.

5. another word for the permanent character you receive

Catholic beliefs and practices

Living Our Faith

As believers in Jesus Christ, we are called to a new life and to make moral choices that keep us united with God. With the help and grace of the Holy Spirit, we can choose ways to act to remain friends with God, to help other people, and to fulfill our prophetic mission to be witnesses to Christ in all circumstances and at the very heart of the human community.

The Ten Commandments

The Ten Commandments are a special expression of natural law made known to us by God's Revelation and by human reason. They guide us in making choices that allow us to live as God wants us to live. The first three commandments tell us how to love God; the rest show us how to love our neighbor.

Moses with Ten Commandments.

1. I am the Lord your God: you shall not have strange gods before me.

2. You shall not take the name of the Lord your God in vain.

3. Remember to keep holy the Lord's Day.

4. Honor your father and your mother.

5. You shall not kill.

6. You shall not commit adultery.

7. You shall not steal.

8. You shall not bear false witness against your neighbor.

9. You shall not covet your neighbor's wife.

10. You shall not covet your neighbor's goods.

The Great Commandment

The Ten Commandments are fulfilled in Jesus' Great Commandment: "You shall love the Lord your God with all your heart, with all your soul, with all your mind, and with all your strength. . . . You shall love your neighbor as yourself." (Mark 12:30–31)

The New Commandment

Before his death on the cross, Jesus gave his disciples a new commandment: "[L]ove one another. As I have loved you, so you also should love one another." (John 13:34)

Sermon on the Mount, **15th Century.**

The Beatitudes

The Beatitudes are the teachings of Jesus in the Sermon on the Mount. (Matthew 5:3–10)

Jesus teaches us that if we live according to the Beatitudes, we will live a happy Christian life. The Beatitudes fulfill God's promises made to Abraham and his descendants and describe the rewards that will be ours as loyal followers of Christ.

Blessed are the poor in spirit,
for theirs is the kingdom of heaven.

Blessed are they who mourn,
for they will be comforted.

Blessed are the meek,
for they will inherit the land.

Blessed are they who hunger and thirst
for righteousness,
for they will be satisfied.

Blessed are the merciful,
for they will be shown mercy.

Blessed are the clean of heart,
for they will see God.

Blessed are the peacemakers,
for they will be called children of God.

Blessed are they who are persecuted
for the sake of righteousness,
for theirs is the kingdom of heaven.

Works of Mercy

The Corporal and Spiritual Works of Mercy are actions that extend God's compassion and mercy to those in need.

Corporal Works of Mercy

The Corporal Works of Mercy are kind acts by which we help our neighbors with their material and physical needs. They include

feed the hungry

give drink to the thirsty

clothe the naked

shelter the homeless

visit the sick

visit the imprisoned

bury the dead

Spiritual Works of Mercy

The Spiritual Works of Mercy are acts of compassion that serve people's emotional and spiritual needs. They include

instruct	**admonish**
counsel	**comfort**
forgive	**bear wrongs patiently**
pray for others	

Precepts of the Church

The Precepts of the Church describe the minimum effort we must make in prayer and in living a moral life. All Catholics are called to move beyond the minimum by growing in love of God and love of neighbor. The Precepts are as follows:

1. attendance at Mass on Sundays and Holy Days of Obligation

2. confession of sins at least once a year

3. reception of Holy Communion at least once a year during the Easter season

4. observance of the days of fast and abstinence

5. providing for the needs of the Church

Days of Fast
(for Adults)

Ash Wednesday   **Good Friday**

Days of Abstinence
(for all those over 14)

Ash Wednesday   **All Fridays in Lent**

Holy Days of Obligation

Holy Days of Obligation are the days other than Sundays on which we celebrate the great things God has done for us through Jesus and the saints. On Holy Days of Obligation, Catholics are obliged to attend Mass. Six Holy Days of Obligation are celebrated in the United States.

Mary, Mother of God
January 1

Ascension
Forty days after Easter (for those dioceses that do not celebrate the Ascension on the seventh Sunday of Easter)

Assumption of the Blessed Virgin Mary
August 15

All Saints
November 1

Immaculate Conception
December 8

Nativity of Our Lord Jesus Christ
December 25

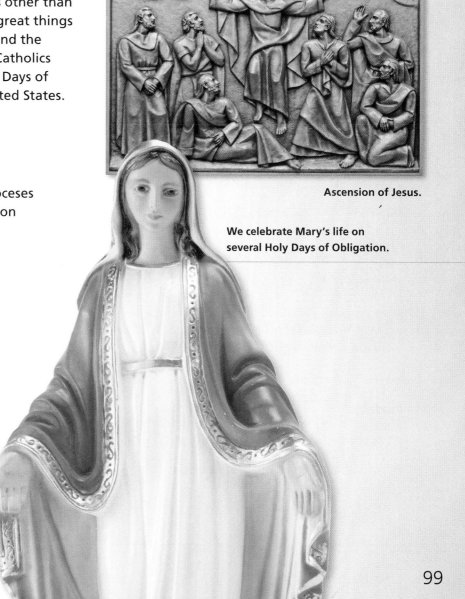

Ascension of Jesus.

We celebrate Mary's life on several Holy Days of Obligation.

Virtues

Virtues are gifts from God that lead us to live in a close relationship with him. Virtues are like good habits. They need to be used; they can be lost if they are neglected. The three most important virtues are called the Theological Virtues because they come from God and lead to God. The Cardinal Virtues are human virtues, acquired by education and good actions. They are named for the Latin word for "hinge" *(cardo),* meaning "that on which other things depend."

Theological Virtues

faith	charity	hope

Cardinal Virtues

prudence	justice
fortitude	temperance

Gifts of the Holy Spirit

The Holy Spirit makes it possible for us to do what God the Father asks of us by giving us many gifts. They include the following:

wisdom	counsel
knowledge	understanding
fortitude	fear of the Lord
piety	

Fruits of the Holy Spirit

The Fruits of the Holy Spirit are examples of the way we find ourselves acting because God is alive in us. They include the following:

love	joy	peace
kindness	generosity	goodness
gentleness	self-control	modesty
faithfulness	chastity	patience

Left to right: the Theogical Virtues of charity, faith, and hope, Heinrich Maria von Hess, 1819.

Making Good Choices

Our conscience is the inner voice that helps us know the law God has placed in our hearts. Our conscience helps us judge the moral qualities of our own actions. It guides us to do good and avoid evil.

The Holy Spirit can help us form a good conscience. We form our conscience by studying the teachings of the Church and following the guidance of our parents and pastoral leaders.

God has given every human being freedom of choice. This does not mean that we have the right to do whatever we please. We can live in true freedom if we cooperate with the Holy Spirit, who gives us the virtue of prudence. This virtue helps us recognize what is good in every situation and make correct choices. The Holy Spirit gives us the gifts of wisdom and understanding to help us make the right choices in life, in relationship to God and others. The gift of counsel helps us reflect on making the correct choices in life.

Showing Our Love for the World

In the story of the Good Samaritan (Luke 10:29–37), Jesus makes clear our responsibility to care for those in need. The Catholic Church teaches this responsibility in the following themes of Catholic Social Teaching.

Life and Dignity of the Human Person

All human life is sacred, and all people must be respected and valued over material goods. We are called to ask whether our actions as a society respect or threaten the life and dignity of the human person.

Call to Family, Community, and Participation

Participation in family and community is central to our faith and a healthy society. Families must be supported so that people can participate in society, build a community spirit, and promote the well-being of all, especially those who are poor and vulnerable.

Rights and Responsibilities

Every person has a right to life as well as a right to those things required for human decency. As Catholics, we have a responsibility to protect these basic human rights in order to achieve a healthy society.

Option for the Poor and Vulnerable

In our world, many people are very rich while at the same time many are extremely poor. As Catholics, we are called to pay special attention to the needs of the poor by defending and promoting their dignity and meeting their immediate material needs.

The Dignity of Work and the Rights of Workers

The Catholic Church teaches that the basic rights of workers must be respected: the right to productive work, fair wages, and private property; and the right to organize, join unions, and pursue economic opportunity. Catholics believe that the economy is meant to serve people and that work is not merely a way to make a living, but an important way in which we participate in God's creation.

Solidarity

Because God is our Father, we are all brothers and sisters with the responsibility to care for one another. Solidarity is the attitude that leads Christians to share spiritual and material goods. Solidarity unites rich and poor, weak and strong, and helps create a society that recognizes that we all depend on one another.

Care for God's Creation

God is the Creator of all people and all things, and he wants us to enjoy his creation. The responsibility to care for all God has made is a requirement of our faith.

Celebrating Our Faith

Jesus touches our lives through the sacraments. In the sacraments, physical objects—water, bread and wine, oil, and others—are the signs of Jesus' presence.

The Seven Sacraments

Sacraments of Initiation

These sacraments lay the foundation of every Christian life.

Baptism

In Baptism we are born into new life in Christ. Baptism takes away Original Sin and makes us members of the Church. One of its signs is the pouring of water.

Confirmation

Confirmation seals our life of faith in Jesus. Its signs are the laying on of hands on a person's head, most often by a bishop, and the anointing with oil. Like Baptism, it is received only once.

Eucharist

The Eucharist nourishes our life of faith. We receive the Body and Blood of Christ under the appearance of bread and wine.

Sacraments of Healing

These sacraments celebrate the healing power of Jesus.

Penance and Reconciliation

Through Reconciliation we receive God's forgiveness. Forgiveness requires being sorry for our sins. In Reconciliation we receive Jesus' healing grace through absolution by the priest. The signs of this sacrament are our confession of sins, our repentance and satisfaction, and the words of absolution.

Anointing of the Sick

This sacrament unites a sick person's sufferings with those of Jesus. Oil, a symbol of strength, is a sign of this sacrament. A person is anointed with oil and receives the laying on of hands from a priest.

Sacraments at the Service of Communion

These sacraments help us serve the community.

Matrimony

In Matrimony a baptized man and woman are united with each other as a sign of the unity between Jesus and his Church. Matrimony requires the consent of the couple, as expressed in the marriage promises. The couple are the sign of this sacrament.

Holy Orders

In Holy Orders, men are ordained priests to be leaders of the community, or deacons to be reminders of our baptismal call to serve others. The signs of this sacrament are the laying on of hands and the prayer of the bishop asking God for the outpouring of the Holy Spirit.

Reconciling with God and Others

An Examination of Conscience

An examination of conscience is the act of prayerfully looking into our hearts to ask how we have hurt our relationships with God and other people through our thoughts, words, and actions. We reflect on the Ten Commandments and the teachings of the Church. The questions below will help us in our examination of conscience.

My Relationship with God

- What steps am I taking to help myself grow closer to God and others? Do I turn to God often during the day, especially when I am tempted?

- Do I participate at Mass with attention and devotion on Sundays and Holy Days? Do I pray often and read the Bible?

- Do I use God's name or the name of Jesus, Mary, and the saints with love and reverence?

My Relationship with Family, Friends, and Neighbors

- Have I set a bad example through my words or actions? Do I treat others fairly? Do I spread stories that hurt other people?

- Am I loving of those in my family? Am I respectful to my neighbors, friends, and those in authority?

- Do I show respect for my body and for the bodies of others? Do I keep away from forms of entertainment that do not respect God's gift of sexuality?

- Have I taken or damaged anything that did not belong to me? Have I cheated, copied homework, or lied?

- Do I quarrel with others just so I can get my own way? Do I insult others to try to make them think they are less than I am? Do I hold grudges and try to hurt people who I think have hurt me?

How to Make a Good Confession

An examination of conscience is an important part of preparing for the Sacrament of Reconciliation. The Sacrament of Reconciliation includes the following steps:

1. The priest greets us and we pray the Sign of the Cross. He may read God's Word with us.

2. We confess our sins. The priest may help and counsel us.

3. The priest gives us a penance to perform. Our penance may be prayers to be prayed, an act of kindness, or both.

4. The priest asks us to express our sorrow, usually by reciting the Act of Contrition.

5. We receive absolution. The priest says, "I absolve you from your sins in the name of the Father, and of the Son, and of the Holy Spirit." We respond, "Amen."

6. The priest dismisses us by saying, "Go in peace." We go forth to perform the act of penance he has given us.

The Eucharist

Sunday is the day on which we celebrate the Resurrection of Jesus. Sunday is the Lord's Day. We gather for Mass, rest from work, and perform Works of Mercy. People from all over the world gather at God's Eucharistic table as brothers and sisters on the Lord's Day.

The Order of Mass

The Mass is the high point of the Christian life, and it always follows a set order.

Introductory Rites

We prepare to celebrate the Eucharist.

Entrance Chant

We gather as a community praising God in song.

Greeting

We pray the Sign of the Cross, recognizing the presence of Christ in the community.

Penitential Act

We acknowledge our sins and ask God for mercy.

Gloria

We praise God in song.

Collect Prayer

The priest gathers all our prayers into one.

Liturgy of the Word

We hear the story of God's plan for Salvation.

First Reading

We listen to God's Word, usually from the Old Testament.

Responsorial Psalm

We respond to God's Word, usually in song.

Second Reading

We listen to God's Word from the New Testament.

Gospel Acclamation

We sing or pray "Alleluia!" to praise God for the Good News. During Lent a different acclamation is used.

Gospel Reading

We stand to acclaim Christ present in the Gospel.

Homily

The priest or deacon explains God's Word.

Profession of Faith

We proclaim our faith through the Creed.

Prayer of the Faithful

We pray for our needs and the needs of others.

Liturgy of the Eucharist

We celebrate the meal that Jesus instituted at the Last Supper and remember the sacrifice he made for us.

Presentation and Preparation of the Gifts

We bring gifts of bread and wine to the altar.

Prayer over the Offerings

The priest prays that God will accept our sacrifice.

Eucharistic Prayer
This prayer of thanksgiving is the center and high point of the entire celebration.

Preface Dialogue
We give thanks and praise to God.

Preface Acclamation
(or Holy, Holy, Holy)
We sing an acclamation of praise.

Institution Narrative
The bread and wine truly become the Body and Blood of Jesus Christ.

The Mystery of Faith
We proclaim Jesus' Death and Resurrection.

Communion Rite
We prepare to receive the Body and Blood of Jesus Christ.

The Lord's Prayer
We pray the Lord's Prayer.

Sign of Peace
We offer one another Christ's peace.

Lamb of God
We pray for forgiveness, mercy, and peace.

Communion
We receive the Body and Blood of Jesus Christ.

Prayer after Communion
We pray that the Eucharist will strengthen us to live as Jesus Christ did.

Amen, Laura James, 2010.

Concluding Rites
At the conclusion of Mass, we are blessed and sent forth.

Final Blessing
We receive God's blessing.

Dismissal
We go in peace to glorify the Lord in our lives.

Devotions of Our Faith

Prayers to Take to Heart

We can pray with any words that come to mind. Sometimes, when we find that choosing our own words is difficult, we can use traditional prayers. Likewise, when we pray aloud with others, we rely on traditional prayers to unite our minds, hearts, and voices. Memorizing traditional prayers such as the following can be very helpful. When we memorize prayers, we take them to heart, meaning that we not only learn the words but also try to understand and live them.

Sign of the Cross

In the name of the Father
and of the Son
and of the Holy Spirit.
Amen.

Lord's Prayer

Our Father, who art in heaven,
hallowed be thy name;
thy kingdom come,
thy will be done
on earth as it is in heaven.
Give us this day our daily bread,
and forgive us our trespasses,
as we forgive those who trespass against us;
and lead us not into temptation,
but deliver us from evil.
Amen.

Glory Be to the Father

Glory be to the Father
and to the Son
and to the Holy Spirit,
as it was in the beginning
is now, and ever shall be
world without end.
Amen.

Hail Mary

Hail, Mary, full of grace,
the Lord is with thee.
Blessed art thou among women
and blessed is the fruit of thy womb, Jesus.
Holy Mary, Mother of God,
pray for us sinners,
now and at the hour of our death.
Amen.

Morning Prayer

God, our Father, I offer you today all that I
    think and do and say.
I offer it with what was done on earth
by Jesus Christ, your Son.
Amen.

Grace Before Meals

Bless us, O Lord, and these thy gifts,
which we are about to receive from thy bounty,
through Christ our Lord.
Amen.

Grace After Meals

We give thee thanks, for all thy benefits,
Almighty God, who live and reign for ever.
And may the souls of the faithful departed,
through the mercy of God, rest in peace.
Amen.

prayers

Nicene Creed

I believe in one God,
the Father almighty,
maker of heaven and earth,
of all things visible and invisible.

I believe in one Lord Jesus Christ,
the Only Begotten Son of God,
born of the Father before all ages.
God from God, Light from Light,
true God from true God,
begotten, not made, consubstantial with
   the Father;
through him all things were made.
For us men and for our salvation
he came down from heaven,
and by the Holy Spirit was incarnate of the
   Virgin Mary,
and became man.

For our sake he was crucified under
   Pontius Pilate,
he suffered death and was buried,
and rose again on the third day
in accordance with the Scriptures.
He ascended into heaven
and is seated at the right hand of the Father.
He will come again in glory
to judge the living and the dead
and his kingdom will have no end.

I believe in the Holy Spirit, the Lord,
   the giver of life,
who proceeds from the Father and the Son,
who with the Father and the Son is adored
   and glorified,
who has spoken through the prophets.

I believe in one, holy, catholic and
   apostolic Church.
I confess one Baptism for the forgiveness of sins
and I look forward to the resurrection
   of the dead
and the life of the world to come.
Amen.

The Apostles' Creed

I believe in God,
the Father almighty,
Creator of heaven and earth,
and in Jesus Christ, his only Son, our Lord,
who was conceived by the Holy Spirit,
born of the Virgin Mary,
suffered under Pontius Pilate,
was crucified, died and was buried;
he descended into hell;
on the third day he rose again from the dead;
he ascended into heaven,
and is seated at the right hand of God the
   Father almighty;
from there he will come to judge the living
   and the dead.

I believe in the Holy Spirit,
the holy catholic Church,
the communion of saints,
the forgiveness of sins,
the resurrection of the body,
and life everlasting.
Amen.

Act of Faith

O my God, I
firmly believe
that you are one God in
three divine Persons,
Father, Son, and
Holy Spirit.
I believe that your divine
Son became man
and died for our sins
and that he will come
to judge the living
and the dead.
I believe these and all the truths
which the Holy Catholic Church teaches
because you have revealed them
who are eternal truth and wisdom,
who can neither deceive nor be deceived.
In this faith I intend to live and die.
Amen.

Act of Hope

O Lord God,
I hope by your grace for the pardon
of all my sins
and after life here to gain eternal happiness
because you have promised it
who are infinitely powerful, faithful, kind,
and merciful.
In this hope I intend to live and die.
Amen.

Act of Love

O Lord God, I love you above all things
and I love my neighbor for your sake
because you are the highest, infinite and
perfect good, worthy of all my love.
In this love I intend to live and die.
Amen.

Prayer to the Holy Spirit

Come, Holy Spirit, fill the hearts of
your faithful.
And kindle in them the fire of your love.
Send forth your Spirit and they shall be created.
And you shall renew the face of the earth.

Let us pray:
O God, by the light of the Holy Spirit
you have taught the hearts of your faithful.
In the same Spirit, help us to know what is
truly right and always to rejoice in your
consolation. We ask this through Christ,
Our Lord.
Amen.

Act of Contrition

O my God, I am heartily sorry for having
offended Thee, and I detest all my sins because
of thy just punishments, but most of all
because they offend Thee, my God, who art
all good and deserving of all my love. I firmly
resolve with the help of Thy grace to sin no
more and to avoid the near occasion of sin.
Amen.

Angelus

V. The angel of the Lord declared unto Mary.

R. And she conceived of the Holy Spirit.

Hail, Mary, full of grace, . . .

V. Behold the handmaid of the Lord.

R. Be done unto me according to thy word.

Hail Mary.

V. And the Word was made flesh.

R. And dwelt among us.

Hail Mary.

V. Pray for us, O holy Mother of God.

R. That we may be made worthy of the promises of Christ.

Let us pray;
Pour forth, we beseech thee, O Lord, thy grace into our hearts; that we, to whom the Incarnation of Christ, thy Son, was made known by the message of an angel, may by his Passion and Cross be brought to the glory of his Resurrection. Through the same Christ, our Lord.
Amen.

Queen of Heaven (Regina Caeli)

Queen of heaven, rejoice, alleluia.
The Son whom you merited to bear, alleluia,
has risen as he said, alleluia.
Rejoice and be glad, O Virgin Mary, alleluia!
For the Lord has truly risen, alleluia.

Let us pray;
O God, who through the resurrection of your Son, our Lord Jesus Christ, did vouchsafe to give joy to the world; grant, we beseech you, that through his Mother, the Virgin Mary, we may obtain the joys of everlasting life. Through the same Christ our Lord.
Amen.

Hail, Holy Queen (Salve Regina)

Hail, Holy Queen, Mother of Mercy,
our life, our sweetness and our hope.
To you do we cry,
poor banished children of Eve.
To you we send up our sighs,
mourning and weeping in this valley
of tears.
Turn then, most gracious advocate,
your eyes of mercy toward us,
and after this exile
show unto us the blessed fruit of thy womb,
Jesus.
O clement, O loving,
O sweet Virgin Mary.

Memorare

Remember, O most gracious Virgin Mary,
that never was it known
that anyone who fled to thy protection,
implored thy help,
or sought thy intercession,
was left unaided.
Inspired by this confidence,
I fly unto thee,
O Virgin of virgins, my Mother.
To thee do I come,
before thee I stand,
sinful and sorrowful.
O Mother of the Word Incarnate,
despise not my petitions,
but in thy mercy hear and
answer me.
Amen.

Praying the Rosary

The Rosary helps us pray to Jesus through Mary. When we pray the Rosary, we think about the special events, or mysteries, in the lives of Jesus and Mary.

The Rosary is made up of a string of beads and a crucifix. We hold the crucifix in our hand as we pray the Sign of the Cross. Then we pray the Apostles' Creed.

Following the crucifix there is a single bead, followed by a set of three beads and another single bead. We pray the Lord's Prayer as we hold the first single bead, and a Hail Mary at each bead in the set of three that follows. Then we pray the Glory Be to the Father. On the next single bead, we think about the first mystery and pray the Lord's Prayer.

There are 5 sets of 10 beads; each set is called a decade. We pray a Hail Mary on each bead of a decade as we reflect on a particular mystery in the lives of Jesus and Mary. The Glory Be to the Father is prayed at the end of each decade. Between decades is a single bead on which we think about one of the mysteries and pray the Lord's Prayer. We end by holding the crucifix in our hands as we pray the Sign of the Cross.

9. Pray ten Hail Marys and one Glory Be to the Father.

10. Think about the fourth mystery. Pray the Lord's Prayer.

8. Think about the third mystery. Pray the Lord's Prayer.

11. Pray ten Hail Marys and one Glory Be to the Father.

7. Pray ten Hail Marys and one Glory Be to the Father.

12. Think about the fifth mystery. Pray the Lord's Prayer.

6. Think about the second mystery. Pray the Lord's Prayer.

5. Pray ten Hail Marys and one Glory Be to the Father.

13. Pray ten Hail Marys and one Glory Be to the Father.

4. Think about the first mystery. Pray the Lord's Prayer.

Pray the Hail, Holy Queen. Many people pray the Hail, Holy Queen after the last decade.

3. Pray three Hail Marys and one Glory Be to the Father.

2. Pray the Lord's Prayer.

14. Pray the Sign of the Cross.

1. Pray the Sign of the Cross and the Apostles' Creed.

The Mysteries of the Rosary

The Church has used three sets of mysteries for many years. In 2002 Pope John Paul II proposed a fourth set of mysteries, the Mysteries of Light, or the Luminous Mysteries. According to his suggestion, the mysteries might be prayed on the following days: the Joyful Mysteries on Monday and Saturday, the Sorrowful Mysteries on Tuesday and Friday, the Glorious Mysteries on Wednesday and Sunday, and the Luminous Mysteries on Thursday.

The Joyful Mysteries

1. **The Annunciation**
   Mary learns that she has been chosen to be the mother of Jesus.

2. **The Visitation**
   Mary visits Elizabeth, who tells Mary that she will always be remembered.

3. **The Nativity**
   Jesus is born in a stable in Bethlehem.

4. **The Presentation**
   Mary and Joseph bring the infant Jesus to the Temple to present him to God.

5. **The Finding of Jesus in the Temple**
   Jesus is found in the Temple discussing his faith with the teachers.

The Luminous Mysteries

1. **The Baptism of Jesus in the River Jordan**
   God the Father proclaims that Jesus is his beloved Son.

2. **The Wedding Feast at Cana**
   At Mary's request, Jesus performs his first miracle.

3. **The Proclamation of the Kingdom of God**
   Jesus calls all to conversion and service to the kingdom.

4. **The Transfiguration of Jesus**
   Jesus is revealed in glory to Peter, James, and John.

5. **The Institution of the Eucharist**
   Jesus offers his Body and Blood at the Last Supper.

The Sorrowful Mysteries

1. **The Agony in the Garden**
   Jesus prays in the Garden of Gethsemane on the night before he dies.

2. **The Scourging at the Pillar**
   Jesus is lashed with whips.

3. **The Crowning with Thorns**
   Jesus is mocked and crowned with thorns.

4. **The Carrying of the Cross**
   Jesus carries the cross that will be used to crucify him.

5. **The Crucifixion**
   Jesus is nailed to the cross and dies.

The Glorious Mysteries

1. **The Resurrection**
   God the Father raises Jesus from the dead.

2. **The Ascension**
   Jesus returns to his Father in Heaven.

3. **The Coming of the Holy Spirit**
   The Holy Spirit comes to bring new life to the disciples.

4. **The Assumption of Mary**
   At the end of her life on earth, Mary is taken body and soul into Heaven.

5. **The Coronation of Mary**
   Mary is crowned as Queen of Heaven and Earth.

Stations of the Cross

The 14 Stations of the Cross represent events from Jesus' Passion and Death. At each station, we use our senses and imaginations to reflect prayerfully on the mystery of Jesus' suffering, Death, and Resurrection.

1

Jesus Is Condemned to Death.
Pontius Pilate condemns Jesus to death.

2

Jesus Takes Up His Cross.
Jesus willingly accepts and patiently bears his cross.

3

Jesus Falls the First Time.
Weakened by torments and loss of blood, Jesus falls beneath his cross.

4

Jesus Meets His Sorrowful Mother.
Jesus meets his mother, Mary, who is filled with grief.

5

Simon of Cyrene Helps Jesus Carry the Cross.
Soldiers force Simon of Cyrene to carry the cross.

6

Veronica Wipes the Face of Jesus.
Veronica steps through the crowd to wipe the face of Jesus.

Continued Next Page

stations

7

Jesus Falls a Second Time.
Jesus falls beneath the weight of the cross a second time.

8

Jesus Meets the Women of Jerusalem.
Jesus tells the women not to weep for him but for themselves and their children.

9

Jesus Falls the Third Time.
Weakened almost to the point of death, Jesus falls a third time.

10

Jesus Is Stripped of His Garments.
The soldiers strip Jesus of his garments, treating him as a common criminal.

11

Jesus Is Nailed to the Cross.
Jesus' hands and feet are nailed to the cross.

12

Jesus Dies on the Cross.
After suffering greatly on the cross, Jesus bows his head and dies.

13

Jesus Is Taken Down from the Cross.
The lifeless body of Jesus is tenderly placed in the arms of Mary, his mother.

14

Jesus Is Laid in the Tomb.
Jesus' disciples place his body in the tomb.

The closing prayer—sometimes included as a 15th station—reflects on the Resurrection of Jesus.

glossary

A

absolution the forgiveness we receive from God through the priest in the Sacrament of Penance and Reconciliation. Absolution places us in the state of grace and ready to receive other sacraments.

Advocate Jesus' name for the Holy Spirit. The Holy Spirit comforts us, speaks for us in difficult times, and makes Jesus present to us.

apostolic the Mark of the Church that indicates that Jesus continues to lead the Church through the pope and the bishops. The pope and the bishops are the successors of the Apostles.

Assumption Mary's being taken, body and soul, into Heaven. Mary had a special relationship with her Son, Jesus, from the very beginning when she conceived him. Because of this relationship, she enjoys a special participation in Jesus' Resurrection and has been taken into Heaven where she now lives with him. We celebrate this event in the Feast of the Assumption on August 15.

B

Beatitudes the teachings of Jesus in the Sermon on the Mount in Matthew's Gospel. The Beatitudes are eight ways of living the Christian life. They are the fulfillment of the commandments given to Moses. These teachings present the way to true happiness.

C

Cardinal Virtues the four virtues that help a person live in relationship with God and others: prudence, justice, fortitude, and temperance.

catholic one of the four Marks of the Church. The Church is catholic because Jesus is fully present in it, because it proclaims the fullness of faith, and because Jesus has given the Church to the whole world. The Church is universal.

charity a virtue given to us by God that helps us love God above all things and our neighbor as ourselves

chastity being faithful to one's sexuality in conduct and intention. Chastity helps us live out our sexuality in a proper manner.

Chrism a perfumed oil, consecrated by a bishop, that is used in the Sacraments of Baptism, Confirmation, and Holy Orders. Anointing with Chrism signifies the call of the baptized to the threefold ministry of priest, prophet, and king.

Christ a title that means "anointed one." It is from a Greek word that means the same thing as the Hebrew word *Messiah,* or "anointed." It is the name given to Jesus as priest, prophet, and king.

Church the people of God throughout the whole world, the people of a diocese (the local Church), or the assembly of those called together to worship God. The Church is one, holy, catholic, and apostolic.

Collect the opening prayer at Mass or other liturgy. A collect is addressed to God and asks for God's presence and grace.

conscience the inner voice that helps each of us judge the morality of our own actions. It guides us to follow God's law by doing good and avoiding evil.

Corporal Works of Mercy kind acts by which we help our neighbors with their everyday, material needs. Corporal Works of Mercy include feeding the hungry, finding a home for the homeless, clothing the naked, visiting the sick and those in prison, giving alms to the poor, and burying the dead.

counsel the gift of the Holy Spirit that helps seek advice and accept the advice of others. Counsel is also known as right judgment.

D

disciple a person who has decided to follow the teachings of Jesus and live them every day

E

Ecumenism the movement to bring unity to separated Christian denominations

F

faith a gift of God that helps us believe in him. We profess our faith in the Creed, celebrate it in the sacraments, live by it through our good conduct of loving God and our neighbor, and express it in prayer. It is a personal adherence of the whole person to God, who has revealed himself to us through words and actions throughout history.

faithfulness the fruit of the Holy Spirit seen in our ability to keep promises and remain loyal to God and those to whom we are committed

fear of the Lord the gift of the Holy Spirit that helps us recognize God's greatness and our dependence on him. The gift of fear of the Lord is sometimes called wonder and awe.

fortitude the strength to choose to do the right thing even when that is difficult. Fortitude is one of the four central human virtues, called the Cardinal Virtues, by which we guide our conduct through faith and the use of reason. Fortitude is also one of the Gifts of the Holy Spirit that gives us the ability to live as a follower of Jesus, stand up for our beliefs, and live a good Christian life.

Fruits of the Holy Spirit the demonstration through our actions that God is alive in us. Saint Paul lists the Fruits of the Holy Spirit in Galatians 5:22–23: love, joy, peace, patience, kindness, generosity, faithfulness, gentleness, and self-control. Church Tradition has added goodness, modesty, and chastity to make a total of 12.

G

generosity the fruit of the Holy Spirit seen in the willingness to give even when at one's own cost

gentleness the fruit of the Holy Spirit seen in the ability to be gracious, peaceful, and forgiving instead of being rough or angry

Gifts of the Holy Spirit the permanent willingness, given to us through the Holy Spirit, that makes it possible for us to do what God asks of us. The Gifts of the Holy Spirit are drawn from Isaiah 11:1–3. They include wisdom, understanding, right judgment, courage, knowledge, and wonder and awe. Church Tradition has added reverence to make a total of seven.

goodness the fruit of the Holy Spirit seen in our love for all people and our loving actions toward them

grace the gift of God, given to us without our meriting it. Grace is the Holy Spirit alive in us, helping us live our Christian vocation. Grace helps us live as God wants us to.

H

holy the Mark of the Church that indicates that the Church is one with Jesus Christ. Holiness is closeness to God, and therefore the Church is holy because God is present in it.

hope the confidence that God will always be with us, make us happy now and forever, and help us live so that we will be with him forever

I

Immaculate Conception the Church teaching that Mary was free from Original Sin from the first moment of her conception. She was preserved through the merits of her Son, Jesus, the Savior of the human race. It was declared a dogma of the Catholic Church by Pope Pius IX in 1854 and is celebrated on December 8.

indelible the quality of being permanent and unable to be erased or undone. The Sacraments of Baptism, Confirmation, and Holy Orders have an indelible character.

infallible the inability to be in error or to teach something that is false. On matters of belief and morality, the Church is infallible because of the presence and guidance of the Holy Spirit. The pope, in union with the bishops, can teach infallibly on matters of faith and morals.

J

joy a deep and constant gladness in the Lord that circumstances cannot destroy. It comes from a good relationship with God and others—a relationship of genuine love.

justice the virtue that guides us to give to God and others what is due them. Justice is one of the four central human virtues, called the Cardinal Virtues, by which we guide our Christian life.

K

kindness the fruit of the Holy Spirit seen in generous acts of service to others

Kingdom of God God's rule over us, announced in the Gospels and present in the Eucharist. The beginning of the kingdom here on earth is mysteriously present in the Church, and it will come in completeness at the end of time.

knowledge one of the seven Gifts of the Holy Spirit. This gift helps us know what God asks of us and how we should respond.

L

Last Judgment the final judgment of all human beings that will occur when Christ returns in glory and all appear in their own bodies before him to give an account of all their deeds in life. In the presence of Christ, the truth of each person's relationship with God will be laid bare, as will the good that each person had done or failed to do during his or her earthly life. At that time God's kingdom will come into its fullness.

Liturgy of the Eucharist the part of Mass in which the bread and wine are consecrated and become the Body and Blood of Jesus Christ. We then receive Christ in Holy Communion.

Liturgy of the Word the part of Mass in which we listen to God's Word from the Bible and consider what it means for us today. The Liturgy of the Word can also be a public prayer and proclamation of God's Word that is not followed by the Liturgy of the Eucharist.

love the fruit of the Holy Spirit, also called *charity,* seen in selfless acts of care and service toward others

M

Magisterium the living, teaching office of the Church. This office, through the bishops and with the pope, provides an authentic interpretation of the Word of God. It ensures faithfulness to the teaching of the Apostles in matters of faith and morals.

Messiah a title that means "anointed one." It is from a Hebrew word that means the same thing as the Hebrew word *Christ*. Messiah is the title given to Jesus as priest, prophet, and king.

modesty the fruit of the Holy Spirit seen in the ability to be moderate and controlled in our actions, especially our conversation and physical appearance.

mortal sin a serious decision to turn away from God by doing something that we know is wrong. For a sin to be mortal, it must be a very serious offense, the person must know how serious it is, and the person must freely choose to do it anyway.

N

Nicene Creed the summary of Christian beliefs developed by the bishops at the first two councils of the Church held in A.D. 325 and 381. It is the Creed shared by most Christians, in the East and in the West.

O

one one of the four Marks of the Church. The Church is one because of its source in the one God and because of its founder, Jesus Christ. Jesus, through his Death on the cross, united all to God in one body.

Original Sin the consequence of the disobedience of the first human beings. They disobeyed God and chose to follow their own will rather than God's will. As a result, human beings lost the original blessing God had intended and became subject to sin and death. In Baptism we are restored to life with God through Jesus Christ although we still experience the effects of Original Sin.

P

particular judgment a judgment made by Christ received by every person at the moment of death that offers either entrance into heaven (after a period of purification, if needed) or immediate and eternal separation from God in hell. At the moment of death, each person is rewarded by Christ in accordance with his or her works and faith.

Paschal Mystery the work of salvation accomplished by Jesus Christ through his Passion, Death, Resurrection, and Ascension. The Paschal Mystery is celebrated in the liturgy of the Church, and we experience its saving effects in the sacraments. In every liturgy of the Church, God the Father is blessed and adored as the source of all blessings we have received through his Son in order to make us his children through the Holy Spirit.

patience the fruit of the Holy Spirit seen in enduring love for others despite suffering, difficulties, and disappointments

peace the fruit of the Holy Spirit seen in persons who remain calm and serene without becoming anxious or upset

piety the gift of the Holy Spirit that helps us love and worship God. Piety is also known as reverence.

prudence the virtue that directs us toward the good and helps us to choose the correct means to achieve that good. When we act with prudence, we carefully and thoughtfully consider our actions. Prudence is one of the Cardinal Virtues that guide our conscience and influence us to live according to the Law of Christ.

Purgatory a state of final cleansing of all our human imperfections after death to prepare us to enter into the joy of God's presence in Heaven.

R

Rite of Christian Initiation of Adults (RCIA) the formal process by which adults become members of the Church. RCIA includes different types of spiritual formation that lead to Baptism, Confirmation, and receiving Holy Communion for the first time at the Easter Vigil.

S

sacraments the seven official rites through which God's life enters our lives in the liturgy through the work of the Holy Spirit. Christ's work in the liturgy is sacramental because his mystery is made present there by the power of the Holy Spirit. Jesus gave us three sacraments that bring us into the church: Baptism, Confirmation, and the Eucharist. He gave us two sacraments that bring us healing: Penance and Reconciliation and Anointing of the Sick. He also gave us two sacraments that help members serve the community: Matrimony and Holy Orders.

sanctifying grace the gift of God, given to us without our earning it, that introduces us to the intimacy of the Trinity, unites us with its life, and heals our human nature wounded by sin. Sanctifying grace helps us respond to our vocation as God's adopted children, and it continues the work of making us holy that began at our Baptism.

self-control the fruit of the Holy Spirit seen in the ability to be disciplined in one's desires and respectful of the dignity and integrity of others

Spiritual Works of Mercy the kind acts through which we help our neighbors meet their needs that are more than material. The Spiritual Works of Mercy include instructing, admonishing, counseling, comforting, forgiving, bearing wrongs patiently, and praying for others.

sponsor a person who supports, guides, and presents a person for the Sacrament of Confirmation. A sponsor must be 16 years old, have received the Sacrament of Confirmation, and live a Christian life.

stewardship the careful and responsible management of something entrusted to one's care, especially the goods of creation, which are intended for the whole human race. The sixth Precept of the Church makes clear our part in stewardship by requiring us to provide for the material needs of the Church, according to our abilities.

T

temperance the Cardinal Virtue that helps us control our attraction to pleasure so that our natural desires are kept within proper limits. This moral virtue helps us choose to use created goods in moderation.

Ten Commandments the 10 rules given by God to Moses on Mount Sinai that sum up God's law and show us what is required to love God and our neighbor. By following the Ten Commandments, the Hebrews accepted their Covenant with God.

Theological Virtues the three virtues of faith, hope, and charity that are gifts from God and not acquired by human effort. The virtue of faith helps us believe in him, the virtue of hope helps us desire eternal life and the Kingdom of God, and the virtue of charity helps us love God and our neighbor as we should.

Torah the Hebrew word for "instruction" or "law." It is also the name of the first five books of the Old Testament: Genesis, Exodus, Leviticus, Numbers, and Deuteronomy.

Trinity, Holy the mystery of the existence of God in the three Persons, the Father, the Son, and the Holy Spirit. Each Person is God, whole and entire. Each is distinct only in the relationship of each to the others. We follow Jesus, God the Son, because God the Father calls us and God the Holy Spirit moves us.

U

understanding one of the seven Gifts of the Holy Spirit. This gift helps us make the right choices in life and in our relationships with God and with others.

V

venial sin a choice we make that weakens our relationship with God or other people. Venial sin wounds and lessens the divine life in us. If we make no effort to do better, venial sin can lead to more serious sin. Through our participation in the Eucharist, venial sin is forgiven when we are repentant, strengthening our relationship with God and others.

virtue a firm attitude or way of acting that enables us to do good

W

wisdom one of the seven Gifts of the Holy Spirit. Wisdom helps us understand the purpose and plan of God and live in a way that helps bring about this plan. It begins in wonder and awe at God's greatness.

index

acknowledgments

Excerpts from the *New American Bible, revised edition* © 2010, 1991, 1986, 1970 Confraternity of Christian Doctrine, Washington, D.C. and are used by permission of the copyright owner. All rights reserved. No part of the *New American Bible* may be reproduced in any form without permission in writing from the copyright owner.

Excerpts from the English translation of *Rite of Baptism for Children* © 1969, International Commission on English in the Liturgy Corporation (ICEL); the English translation of the Act of Contrition from *Rite of Penance* © 1974, ICEL; excerpts from the English translation of *Rite of Confirmation (Second Edition)* © 1975, ICEL; the English translation of the *Memorare*, Queen of Heaven, and *Salve Regina* from *A Book of Prayers* © 1982, ICEL; the English translation of the Prayer Before Meals and Prayer After Meals from *Book of Blessings* © 1988, ICEL; the English translation of the Nicene Creed and Apostles' Creed from *The Roman Missal* © 2010, ICEL. All rights reserved.

The Prayer to the Holy Spirit is from the *United States Catholic Catechism for Adults.* © 2006, U.S. Conference of Catholic Bishops. All rights reserved.

Loyola Press has made every effort to locate the copyright holders for the cited works used in this publication and to make full acknowledgment for their use. In the case of any omissions, the publisher will be pleased to make suitable acknowledgments in future editions.

Art and Photography

When there is more than one picture on a page, positions are abbreviated as follows: **(t)** top, **(c)** center, **(b)** bottom, **(l)** left, **(r)** right, **(bg)** background, **(bd)** border.

Photos and illustrations not acknowledged are either owned by Loyola Press or from royalty-free sources including but not limited to Art Resource, Alamy, Bridgeman, Corbis/Veer, Getty Images, iStockphoto, Jupiterimages, Media Bakery, PunchStock, Shutterstock, Thinkstock, and Wikipedia Commons. Loyola Press has made every effort to locate the copyright holders for the cited works used in this publication and to make full acknowledgment for their use. In the case of any omissions, the publisher will be pleased to make suitable acknowledgments in future editions.

Frontmatter: iii iStockphoto/Thinkstock. **iv–v** Colorblind/Media Bakery. **vi** The Crosiers/Gene Plaisted, OSC.

© iStockphoto.com: 6 (t) cstar55. **9** (c) Liliboas. **10** eyedear. **11** (br) blackie. **13** (t) N_design. **14** (b) SimplyCreativePhotography. **15** (b) N_design. **19** (b) sebastianiov. **20** (b) digitalskillet. **25** (t) aerobaby. **31** (b) jaroon. **37** (t) Natural_Warp. **39, 47** (b) Natural_Warp.

40 DOConnell. **42** (b) BriArt. **43** FineCollection. **47** (t) CEFutcher. **49, 51, 59** (br) naddi. **50** Rhoberazzi. **56–57** (b) urbancow. **61, 63, 71** (t) Pingwin. **62** (b) KyleNelson. **69** (c) ericsphotography. **70** splain2me. **71** (l) Pingwin. **73, 75, 83** 77DZIGN. **73** (b) grandriver. **74** (t) grandriver. **74** (b) drbimages. **77** (b) oleg66. **82** fotoVoyager. **83** (l) 77DZIGN. **83** (r) GomezDavid. **85** mxtama. **86** (b) lovleah. **87** (b) mxtama. **88** (b) Okea. **91** (b) sebastianiov. **95** (b) mxtama. **102** (t) iStockphoto.com. **102** Clockwise from upper left: (f) princessdlaf, (g) sebastianiov. **104** princessdlaf. **106** (b) Natural_Warp. **109** LordRunar.

Thinkstock: 1 Digital Vision. **2** (t) Digital Vision. **7** iStockphoto. **7** iStockphoto. **9** (t) iStockphoto. **23** iStockphoto. **24** iStockphoto. **25** (t) Hemera. **25** (t) iStockphoto. **25–26** (b) Jupiterimages/Comstock. **27** (b) iStockphoto. **30** (t) iStockphoto. **34** iStockphoto. **35** (b) iStockphoto. **46** Hemera. **49, 51, 59** (bl) iStockphoto. **54** (b) Stockbyte. **58** iStockphoto. **62** (t) Hemera. **65** (t) Jupiterimages/Photos.com. **71** (r) Thomas Northcut/Photodisc. **76** Zoonar. **90** (b) Hemera. **95** (t) iStockphoto. **108** (b) Sean Murphy/Lifesize.

Chapter 1: 2 (b) Getty Images. **3** (t) He Qi, He Qi Arts, www.heqigallery.com. **4** (t) Loyola Press Photography. **4** (b) Andrew Ward/Life File/Photodisc. **5** (t) Wikipedia. **6** (b) Zulhazmi Zabri/Shutterstock.com. **8** (t) Window of John the Evangelist at St. Mary's Church, Edward Burne-Jones, 1898, Speldhurst, England. The Crosiers/Gene Plaisted, OSC. **8–9** (b) Jupiterimages.

Chapter 2: 13 (b) Fancy/Alamy. **14** (t) Noel Hendrickson/Digital Vision/Getty Images. **15** (t) Private Collection/The Bridgeman Art Library International. **16** (t) W.P. Wittman Limited. **16** (b) Phil Martin Photography. **17** Phil Martin Photography. **18** W.P. Wittman Limited. **19** (t) Phil Martin Photography. **20** (t) Icon of Saint John Neumann, courtesy of Monastery Icons, © 2001, www.monasteryicons.com. **21** Warling Studios. **22** Blend Images Photography/Veer.

Chapter 3: 26 (b) Jupiterimages. **27** (t) Image by Elizabeth Wang, RL Code T-05121-CW-V3, © Radiant Light 2010, www.radiantlight.org.uk. **28** (t) Private Collection/The Bridgeman Art Library International. **28** (b) Loyola Press Photography/www.rosarymarket.com. **29** Design Pics/PunchStock. **31** (t) laurent dambies/Shutterstock.com. **32** (t) Saint Benedict and Saint Scholastica. Zvonimir Atletic/Shutterstock.com. **32–33** (b) David De Lossy/Photodisc/Getty Images. **33** (t) Warling Studios. **33** (c) Loyola Press Photography/www.rosarymarket.com. **35** (t) Corbis Photography/Veer. **36** W.P. Wittman Limited.

Chapter 4: 37 (b) Lawrence Manning/Media Bakery. **38** Karina Bakalyan/Shutterstock.com. **39** (t) Private Collection/The Bridgeman Art Library International. **41** (t) © National Gallery of Scotland, Edinburgh, Scotland/The Bridgeman Art Library International. **42** (t) Phil Martin Photography. **44** (t) Mother Teresa accompanied by children at her mission, Tim Graham, November 27th, 2010, Calcutta, India. Tim Graham/Alamy. **44–45** Alan Burles/Alamy.